PHILOSOPHY
OF THE RECENT PAST

PHILOSOPHY OF THE RECENT PAST

AN OUTLINE OF EUROPEAN AND
AMERICAN PHILOSOPHY SINCE 1860

BY
RALPH BARTON PERRY
PROFESSOR OF PHILOSOPHY IN HARVARD UNIVERSITY

CHARLES SCRIBNER'S SONS
NEW YORK   CHICAGO   BOSTON
ATLANTA   SAN FRANCISCO

COPYRIGHT, 1926, BY
CHARLES SCRIBNER'S SONS

Printed in the United States of America

PREFACE

This book is intended as an introduction to the philosophy which has lately established its place in the record of mankind. To deal both comprehensively and justly with strictly contemporary thought is an impossible task. If I have seemed to slight many notable living philosophers, this does not imply that I regard them as unimportant, but only that I hesitate to anticipate the verdict of history.

I have aimed to set forth each philosophy with sympathetic understanding, rather than to argue my own opinion about it. I hope that through this brief exposition, and through the many references to their works, my readers may find an access to the philosophers themselves—including philosophers of continental Europe as well as of English-speaking countries.

RALPH BARTON PERRY.

CAMBRIDGE, MASS.

CONTENTS

PART I. THE STATE OF PHILOSOPHY IN 1860
- § 1. Germany 2
- § 2. Italy 8
- § 3. France 9
- § 4. Great Britain 12
- § 5. America 16

PART II. NATURALISM, MATERIALISM, AND POSITIVISM
- § 6. Darwin and Darwinism 20
- § 7. Cosmic Evolution. Spencer 29
- § 8. Monism of Substance. Haeckel . . . 38
- § 9. The Rise of Positivism. Comte . . . 43
- § 10. Empirical Positivism. Mill 52
- § 11. Economical Positivism. Lange. Mach. Poincaré 60
- § 12. Sociological Positivism. Durkheim . . 71
- § 13. The Influence of Recent Science . . . 75

PART III. SPIRITUALISM AND IDEALISM
- § 14. Spiritualism in Germany. Fechner. Lotze. Hartmann 81
- § 15. Spiritualism in France. Maine de Biran. Cousin. Ravaisson. Boutroux . . . 97
- § 16. Idealism in France. Renouvier. Lachelier . 113
- § 17. Idealism in England. Green. Bradley. Bosanquet 126

CONTENTS

		PAGE
§ 18.	Idealism in America. Royce. Howison. Bowne	136
§ 19.	Critical Idealism in Germany. Cohen. Natorp	145
§ 20.	Ethical and Cultural Idealism in Germany. Windelband. Rickert. Dilthey. Eucken. Simmel	151
§ 21.	The New Idealism in Italy. Croce. Gentile	160

PART IV. VITALISM, VOLUNTARISM, AND PRAGMATISM

§ 22.	The Will to Power. Nietzsche	168
§ 23.	The Impulse to Life. Bergson	174
§ 24.	Catholic Modernism. Le Roy	183
§ 25.	Pragmatism and the Will to Believe. James. Peirce. Dewey. Schiller. Vaihinger	186

PART V. THE REVIVAL OF REALISM

§ 26.	The Reaction against Idealism	197
§ 27.	Neo-Thomism	201
§ 28.	Realism in Germany. Meinong. Husserl	205
§ 29.	Realism in England and America. Russell. Moore. Alexander. Santayana. Whitehead	211

CONCLUSION

§ 30.	Tendencies of the Immediate Present	221

SELECTED BIBLIOGRAPHY 224

INDEX 227

PHILOSOPHY
OF THE RECENT PAST

PHILOSOPHY OF THE RECENT PAST

PART I

THE STATE OF PHILOSOPHY IN 1860

Schopenhauer, the last representative of the great metaphysical movement inspired directly by the critical philosophy of Kant, died in 1860. A cross-section of European and American philosophy in the years immediately before and after this date reveals both the diversity and diffusion of the post-Kantian metaphysics itself, and the rise of the great rival movement which was to dispute its control during the latter half of the nineteenth century.

The metaphysical impulse communicated by Kant moved in two divergent directions. In his recognition of the thing-in-itself behind appearances, in his provision under the form of faith for God, freedom, and immortality, and in his qualified assent to a purposive and æsthetic interpretation of nature, he encouraged the revival of a *spiritualistic realism* after the manner of Leibniz. In his doctrine of the organizing and creative activity of the knowing mind, through its forms of sensibility, its categories of understanding, and its ideals of reason, he founded modern *idealism*. Each of these varieties of post-Kantian metaphysics proved capable of great diversification in the course of their later history both in Germany and abroad. The rival movement was *naturalism*, or the philosophy inspired by the progress of the physical sciences. This influence of science on philosophy took two forms, according as attention was directed to the content of science or to its form. *Materialism* adapted the content of physics to the purposes of metaphysics, or employed particular scientific theories, such as the conservation of matter and force, or evolution, as an account of reality. *Positivism*, on the other hand, was primarily concerned with the method of science, holding that science alone provided genuine knowledge. This unique cognitive success of science was attributed by some to its close adherence to the facts of experience, and by others to its descriptive technic and satisfaction of human needs. The first of these interpretations of scientific knowledge furnished the motive of *empirical* positivism, and was peculiarly congenial to the tradition of English thought; the second constituted the motive of *economical* positivism, and was relatively characteristic of Germany and France. Naturalism of both varieties turned human hope and aspiration away from the supernatural world and focussed them upon man and *society*. Hence the growth of naturalism was accompanied by the scientific study of society (sociology), and by the formulation of programmes of social reform.

§ 1. Germany

When we turn to the state of GERMAN philosophy in or about the year 1860, its most notable characteristic is undoubtedly the rise of naturalism. This was in part a development within the reigning metaphysical schools. The internal controversy among the Hegelians arose from the general prominence at this time of the issue between philosophy and established religion. DAVID STRAUSS,[1] the leader of the "left" or liberal wing of the Hegelian school, reduced the orthodox dogmas to myths, and contended that the only religion consistent with a strict interpretation of Hegel's teachings was a naturalistic pantheism. LUDWIG FEUERBACH[2] contended that, in view of Hegel's rejection of creation, providence, immortality, and free-will, it could not be justly claimed that he gave philosophical support to popular spiritualism and religious orthodoxy. As his thought developed, Feuerbach identified himself closely with the scientific view of the world, and construed religion as only the imaginative projection of human needs and hopes.[3] This tendency of naturalism to substitute human and social for supernatural values is most conspicuously represented among Hegelians by KARL MARX,[4] whose famous book on *Capital* (*Das Ka-*

[1] In his famous *Leben Jesu* (1835). His most important later writings were *Die christliche Glaubenslehre* (1840–1841) and *Der alte und der neue Glaube* (1872). He has an important place in the history of the philosophy of religion and of biblical criticism.

[2] 1804–1872. The greatest of his works is the *Wesen des Christenthums*, 1841. His *Grundsätze der Philosophie der Zukunft* appeared in 1843, the *Theogonie* in 1857, and the *Gott, Freiheit und Unsterblichkeit* in 1866.

The other important representatives of this group were Arnold Ruge (1802–1880) and Bruno Bauer (1809–1882). The extreme development of Feuerbach's anthropological ethics and religion is represented by the revolutionary individualism of Caspar Schmidt (1806–1856), commonly known under his pseudonym of Max Stirner. His *Der Einzige und sein Eigenthum* (1845) has had great popular vogue.

[3] Feuerbach was the author of the famous dictum, cited at this time as the quintessence of the crassest materialism, that "man is what he eats" (*Man ist was er isst*).

[4] 1818–1883.

pital) was published in 1867, and became the bible of modern socialism. Marx adopted Hegel's historical method and his emphasis on dialectic, construing the former in terms of economic development and the latter in terms of class conflict.

Strauss, Feuerbach, and Marx illustrate the materialistic trend, toward 1860, of Hegelianism, the greatest of the post-Kantian metaphysical schools. But there was also a strong naturalistic motive in Kant himself which had been overruled by his idealistic followers, and which was now revived. Although Kant gave no encouragement to materialism, his *Critique of Pure Reason*, strictly construed, and separated from the *Critique of Practical Reason* and the *Critique of Judgment*, could be cited as an indorsement of positivism; since it set forth the view that science alone fulfils the requirements of knowledge, as uniting the forms of intuition and the categories of the understanding with the data of experience. Hence, in the 1860's, German positivism, as represented by Albert Lange and OTTO LIEBMANN, adopted the shibboleth "Back to Kant," [1] and appealed to the master against his disciples. These thinkers regarded Kant as untrue to his own insight in so far as by his recognition of the thing-in-itself he encouraged the revival of dogmatic metaphysics, and they proposed to limit philosophy to the critical examination of the pre-

---

[1] This exhortation (*Also muss auf Kant zurückgegangen werden!*) appeared at the close of each chapter of Liebmann's *Kant und die Epigonen* (1865). Liebmann was born in 1840 and died in 1912. Lange (§ 11) published his important *History of Materialism* in 1866. With the name of Lange should be associated that of Eugen Dühring (1833–1921), whose *Natürliche Dialektik* appeared in 1865.

suppositions of science. They thus furnished a connecting link between a positivistic naturalism, and the strict Kantianism which came to be known as *neo-criticism* or *critical idealism*.[1]

But while German naturalism may be said to have sprung in part from within the Kantian movement itself, it received its chief impetus at this time from the achievements of science. Although naturalism is inspired by science, it undertakes to satisfy the philosophical demand for a comprehensive view of the world, and is therefore influenced by the *generalizations* of science, rather than by its particular items. Modern naturalism had up to this time appealed mainly in the *mechanical theory* originated by Galileo and perfected by Newton. But in the middle of the nineteenth century the most impressive scientific generalization was that of *conservation*, or the quantitative constancy of both matter and force (or energy) in all their diverse qualitative manifestations. The principle of the conservation of matter had been established by LAVOISIER, the founder of modern chemistry.[2] The principle of the conservation of energy was not generally accepted until the year 1860, as a result of the work of MAYER, JOULE, and HELMHOLZ.[3] The combination of these two prin-

---

[1] § 19.

[2] Antoine Laurent Lavoisier (1743-1794) was a Frenchman and a victim of the Revolution.

[3] Julius Robert Mayer (1814-1874) announced his conclusions in 1842. In his *Die organische Bewegung in ihrem Zusammenhange mit dem Stoffwechsel* (1845) he combined the principle of the conservation of energy with that of matter, in their application to vital processes. James Prescott Joule (1818-1889), an Englishman, announced his conclusions in 1843. Hermann L. F. von Helmholz (1821-1895) published his *Über die Erhaltung der Kraft* in 1847. These scientists together with the Danish

ciples suggested a new type of philosophical monism, in which nature was regarded as a fixed amount of energized matter proceeding in a ceaseless and circular round of change. Life and mind were regarded as parts of this closed system, the organism being one of the forms assumed by matter, and consciousness one of the forms assumed by energy. The most important exposition of this thesis was contained in MOLESCHOTT's *Circulation of Life* (*Der Kreislauf des Lebens*), published in 1852, and it acquired great popular vogue through BÜCHNER's *Force and Matter* (*Kraft und Stoff*), of which sixteen editions appeared in Germany between 1855 and 1889.[1] The bitter controversy to which this movement gave rise was due to its uncompromising denial both of Christian orthodoxy and of common-sense spiritualism.[2]

The counterclaims of spiritualism were championed in Germany at this time by the "right" wing of the Hegelian school, and by the so-called "semi-Hegelians"

---

physicist Colding and the German physicist Mohr appear to have reached their conclusions independently, and their rival claims to priority are still a matter of controversy. The English physicist based his conclusions on experimental research, while the Continental physicists were more influenced by general philosophical considerations, such as the axiom of the equality of cause and effect (*causa æquat effectum*). The new principle must also be viewed as the logical outcome of earlier developments in physics. It is peculiarly an idea of the *times*, rather than of any single individual.

[1] Jacob Moleschott (1822–1893); Louis Büchner (1824–1899). Other leading members of this school were Karl Vogt (1817–1895) and Heinrich Czolbe (1819–1873). Ernst Haeckel (§ 70) continued this tradition, but was distinguished as belonging to a later period by the shift of emphasis from the principle of conservation to that of evolution, resulting from the influence of Darwin.

[2] As illustrated, for example, by Moleschott's famous saying: "No phosphorus, no thought" (*Ohne Phosphor kein Gedanke*).

who sought to correct Hegel and to develop a philosophical basis for theism.[1] But it is a striking fact that the great leaders of the anti-naturalistic movement did not draw their inspiration mainly from Kantian idealism. They were not primarily concerned with the ideality of nature, or its dependence on mind through the act of knowledge, but, rather, with the immanence of mind *in* nature. They were, in short, spiritual realists, who revived the Aristotelian and Leibnizian tradition. They were alienated even from Schopenhauer and Schelling, because, having felt the influence of science, they could not be wholly in sympathy with the romantic and *a priori* method of dealing with nature. Fechner, whose *Zenda Vesta* appeared in 1851, and Lotze, whose *Microcosmos* appeared in 1856, were not only spiritualistic in their metaphysics, but were among the founders of experimental and physiological psychology. The third of the great representatives of this movement[2] was von Hartmann, whose *Philosophy of the Unconscious (Philosophie des Unbewussten)* was published in 1869.

The currents of thought which were characteristic of German philosophy in 1860 were reproduced in Italy, France, England, and America. In these countries as well as in Germany, one finds two major and conflicting tendencies, on the one hand naturalism, either materialistic or positivistic, and on the other hand the anti-naturalistic movement, inclining either to idealism or to a spiritualistic realism.

[1] To this latter group belonged Christian Hermann WEISSE (1801–1866), Karl Philipp Fischer (1807–1885), and Immanuel Hermann Fichte (1797–1879).
[2] § 14.

§ 2. Italy

ITALIAN thought, outside of orthodox Catholicism, was dominated at the opening of the century by the sensationalism and naturalism of the French Revolution. Later influences of the same type were received from Comte, and stimulated the work of ARDIGÒ, the leader of Italian positivism.[1]

Italian spiritualism and idealism were represented toward the middle of the century by ROSMINI and GIOBERTI,[2] who were churchmen and patriots as well as philosophers; and sought, on the one hand, to reconcile Catholicism with modern philosophy by emphasizing the Platonic-idealistic element in Christian thought, and, on the other hand, to give a philosophical and spiritual meaning to Italian national aspirations. They borrowed something of the letter of Kantianism and some of the extravagances of romanticism, but the new critical spirit was inconsistent with the theological and dogmatic tradition which as yet dominated Italian thought. When, after 1848, the nationalistic movement became increasingly secular and anti-traditional, Italian thought became more receptive to the German, and in

---

[1] Roberto Ardigò, 1828–1918. His *La Psicologia come Scienza positiva* appeared in 1871. Giuseppe Ferrari (1811–1876) and Ausonio Franchi (1821–1895) represent the critical and sceptical reaction against both Catholic orthodoxy and the spiritualistic metaphysics.

[2] Antonio Rosmini-Serbati (1797–1855); Vincenzo Gioberti (1801–1852). These are the first Italian philosophers of importance after Giovanni Battista Vico (1668?–1744). Pasquale Gallupi (1770–1846), who slightly preceded them, was influenced by the Scottish school, and in particular by Reid. Their successor was Terenzio Mamiani, a Christian Platonist like themselves, but more free from the influence of dogma and authority.

particular to the Hegelian, influence. This influence was spread after 1860 by the teaching of VERA and SPAVENTA at Naples.¹ At the same time the powerful revival of the scholasticism of Thomas Aquinas was inaugurated by the famous *Philosophia christiana*, published by CAJETANO SANSEVERINO² in 1862. This movement, promoted by the Church, spread rapidly from Italy to Catholic thinkers throughout the world.³

§ 3. France

The philosophical situation in FRANCE in 1860 differed profoundly from that of Germany, owing to the fact that naturalism, so remarkably developed in the closing decades of the eighteenth century, was here the indigenous and established, rather than the innovating, tendency. The naturalism of the Revolutionary period had been carried over into the nineteenth century in two forms. The so-called "idealogues," represented by DESTUTT DE TRACY,⁴ continued to psychologize concerning the origin of ideas after the manner of Condillac and Cabanis. SAINT-SIMON,⁵ on the other hand, gave his attention to a naturalistic philosophy of

---

¹ Augusto Vera (1813–1885) was primarily a translator and expositor of Hegel; cf. his *l'Hégélianisme et la Philosophie*, 1861. Bertrando Spaventa (1817–1883) attempted to free Hegelianism from the odium of a foreign importation and to assimilate it to the Italian tradition; cf. his *La Filosofia di Gioberti*, 1863.

² 1811–1865.

³ § 27.

⁴ 1754–1836: *Œuvres Complètes*, 1824.

⁵ Claude Henri de Rouvroy, Comte de Saint-Simon, 1760–1825: *Œuvres Choisis*, 1859–1861. With Charles Fourier (1772–1837), Pierre Joseph Proudhon (1809–1865), and the Englishman Robert Owen (1771–1858), he belongs to the group of "utopian" or "humanitarian" socialists, with which the history of modern socialism begins.

10 PHILOSOPHY OF THE RECENT PAST

history, to the classification of the sciences, and to social reform. From these sources sprang the French positivistic system of Auguste Comte.[1] This great philosopher had himself passed from the scene in 1857, but his influence, as manifested in LITTRÉ, TAINE, and RENAN,[2] was paramount at the time of the Second Empire in secular and unofficial circles, and has maintained itself steadily down to the present date.

This naturalistic tendency within philosophy proper was reinforced, as in other countries, by the influence of science. Cuvier, Laplace, and Lamarck[3] had given France a position of ascendancy in science at the opening of the century. The eminent physicist AMPÈRE laid

---

[1] § 9.

[2] Maximilien Paul Émile Littré (1801–1881) was an expositor of Comte, though a dissenter from the strict Comtean orthodoxy. His works were: *Analyse raisonnée du Cours de Philosophie positive de M. A. Comte*, 1845; *Application de la Philosophie positive au Gouvernement des Sociétés*, 1849; *Conservation, Révolution et Positivisme*, 1852; *Paroles de Philosophie positive*, 1859; *Auguste Comte et la Philosophie positive*, 1863; *Fragments de Philosophie positive et de Sociologie contemporaine*, 1876. Littré was also the founder of the *Revue positive* (1867–1883), and author of the *Dictionnaire de la Langue française*.

Hippolyte Adolphe Taine (1828–1893; *Les Philosophes français au XIXe Siècle*, 1857; *De l'Intelligence*, 1870) and Ernest Renan (1823–1892; *L'Avenir de Science*, written in 1848, but not published until 1890) were versatile and widely influential thinkers, who developed away from their earlier positivistic position. Taine was a historian and critic of literature and art, while Renan (like his contemporary, David Strauss) was one of the founders of modern biblical criticism. To these names should be added that of Étienne VACHEROT (1809–1897), who emphasized the gulf between the reality revealed in science and the ideal conceived and pursued by man. He was closely related to the "left" of the Hegelian group.

[3] Jean Baptiste Pierre Antoine de Monet, Chevalier de Lamarck, 1744–1829; *Philosophie Zoologique*, 1809. The influence of Lamarck did not make itself felt in French philosophy until the principles of evolution had been given prominence by Darwin and Spencer. Comte and his followers, holding to the discontinuity of nature, rejected the Lamarckian theory of the development of species.

the foundations of modern electromagnetism in 1820,[1] and in the 1860's BERNARD, BERTHELOT, and PASTEUR were continuing this brilliant tradition.[2] But the devotion of French science to the experimental and mathematical method, together with the pervasive spirit of positivism, prevented the appearance in France of the dogmatic materialism which characterized this period in Germany.

Turning to spiritualism and idealism, the extreme reaction, in the name of religious faith and authority, to the excesses of the Revolution, had run its course[3]; and had been superseded by the official and academic philosophy of Cousin, whose famous lectures on *The True, the Beautiful, and the Good* had created a furore in 1818, and who reached the height of his power in the middle of the century. His philosophy was an eclectic spiritualism, derived in part from Scotch realism,[4] in part from Schelling and Hegel, and in part from earlier seventeenth- and eighteenth-century sources.[5] To Cousin was also due the rediscovery of Maine de Biran,[6] who

[1] André Marie Ampère (1775–1836) is characteristic of the close relation between French science and philosophy in the nineteenth century. Ampère was an intimate associate of the "idealogues" and of Maine de Biran, and wrote himself both acutely and voluminously on the origin of ideas and theory of knowledge.

[2] Claude Bernard (1813–1878) and Louis Pasteur (1822–1895) were biologists and physiologists. Pierre Eugène Marcellin Berthelot (1827–1907) was one of the founders of modern physical chemistry.

[3] The most important philosophical representatives of this reactionary tendency, commonly known as "traditionalism," were Joseph de MAISTRE (1754–1821) and Louis Gabriel Ambroise de BONALD (1754–1840).

[4] Through Roger Collard, who introduced Reid in his lectures at the Sorbonne, 1811–1814. Cf. § 15.

[5] Other members of this so-called "Eclectic School" were Théodore Simon JOUFFROY (1796–1842) and Paul JANET (1823–1899).

[6] § 15.

had exercised little influence during his life (1766–1824), but now assumed a position of steadily growing importance in French thought.

As the school of Cousin lost prestige it was superseded in the 1860's by two new movements. The first of these was identified with the name of Renouvier,[1] who began the publication of his *Essais de Critique générale* in 1854, and who, like his German contemporary Lotze, represented not only the Kantian and spiritualistic motives, but the influence of science as well.[2] The second of the new movements was inaugurated by Ravaisson[3] and in particular by his famous *Report on Philosophy in France* (*Rapport sur la Philosophie en France au XIXᵉ Siècle*), prepared in 1867. This work was a résumé and critique of the past, in which the author rejected both positivism and eclecticism; and also an appeal for a new spiritualism, which should be both rigorous in its methods and boldly metaphysical in its results.

§ 4. Great Britain

Turning to the state of BRITISH philosophy in 1860, we find the naturalistic tendency broadly represented by BUCKLE, whose famous *History of Civilization*,[4] founded on the premise of inflexible natural law, was an attempt to interpret history in terms of the physical

[1] § 16.
[2] A similar position is occupied by the mathematician Antoine Augustin COURNOT (1801–1877), who like Renouvier approached philosophy through an examination of the limits of science, but stood closer to Comte. Cf. his *Essai sur les Fondements de nos Connaissances*, 1851, and *Traité de l'Enchaînement des Idées fondamentales*, 1861.
[3] § 15.
[4] Henry Thomas Buckle, 1821–1862. The *History of Civilization* was published in 1857 and 1861.

PHILOSOPHY IN 1860

environment, and progress in terms of the advancement of science. The positivistic movement in Great Britain was represented in 1860 most notably by the positivism of John Stuart Mill, who, following his father, JAMES MILL,[1] continued the empirical tradition of the eighteenth century, and was at the same time related to Comte. Other representatives of this empirical type of positivism were the psychologist and moralist Alexander BAIN,[2] and George Henry LEWES,[3] who interested himself especially in the problem of the relations of mind and body, and who, like J. S. Mill, was influenced by Comte. Somewhat later CLIFFORD,[4] beginning as a zealous and uncompromising advocate of the scientific method, sought in *panpsychism* a method of construing physical nature in terms of experience, and thus of overcoming the dualism of mind and matter.

From the side of science the greatest stimulus to naturalism in England came from the new conception of evolution. If the discoveries of physics were not philosophically fruitful in England at this time it was not for lack of eminent men. DAVY, FARADAY, KELVIN, and MAXWELL,[5] as well as Joule, stood in the foremost ranks of science, and contributed largely to that unified view

---

[1] 1773–1836. He is known as one of the founders of the "associationist" school in psychology (*Analysis of the Phenomena of the Human Mind*, 1829), and as, after Bentham, the leader of the "utilitarian" school in ethics. Cf. § 10.

[2] 1818–1903: *The Senses and the Intellect*, 1855; *The Emotions and the Will*, 1859.

[3] 1817–1878: *Comte's Philosophy of the Positive Sciences*, 1853; *Problems of Life and Mind*, 1874–1879.

[4] William Kingdon Clifford, 1845–1879: *Lectures and Essays*, 1879.

[5] Sir Humphry Davy (1778–1829); Michael Faraday (1791–1867); Lord Kelvin (William Thomson) (1824–1907); James Clerk Maxwell (1831–1879).

of nature as a physico-chemical system which had excited the speculative imagination of the German materialists. But whether because of the anti-metaphysical temper of British thought, or because the conception of evolution appealed more strongly to the spirit of the age and touched human interests more nearly, in any case, the influence of physics was at the time almost wholly eclipsed by that of the biological sciences as represented by Darwin and Spencer.[1] The former's epoch-making work on the *Origin of Species* appeared in 1859. Spencer, to be sure, made much of the principle of the conservation of force and matter, as well as of the results of the new geology,[2] but his own scientific competence lay within the field of the biological and social sciences, and his final synthesis, formulated in 1862 in his *First Principles*, was a law of evolution. In the controversy which the theory of evolution at once precipitated, the most redoubtable controversial champion was HUXLEY,[3] who not only played an important part in the dissemination of the theory, but sought to work out its philosophical presuppositions and moral applications. Associated in the same cause was TYNDALL and afterward ROMANES,[4] who devoted himself to a study of the evolution of mind, and hoped to reconcile Darwinism with religion.

[1] §§ 6, 7.
[2] The so-called "uniformitarian" geology, founded on the work of the mineralogist James Hutton (1726–1797), and developed at this time by Sir Charles Lyell (1797–1875).
[3] Cf. his famous essay on *Man's Place in Nature*, 1863; and his volume on *Hume*, 1878. Thomas Henry Huxley was born in 1825 and died in 1895.
[4] John Tyndall, 1820–1893: *Fragments of Science*, 1871. George John Romanes, 1848–1894: *A Candid Examination of Theism*, 1878; *Mental Evolution in Man*, 1888. Alfred Russel Wallace (1823–1913) arrived independently at conclusions similar to Darwin's in 1858.

PHILOSOPHY IN 1860

The indigenous spiritualistic movement of the Scotch realists, provoked by the sceptical conclusions of Hume, was brought to a close by Sir William HAMILTON and Henry MANSEL,[1] who argued the relativity of all knowledge and hence the impossibility of knowing the "unconditioned"; and who, having thus disposed of every rationalistic metaphysics (including naturalism), defended a spiritualistic and religious belief founded on analogy and faith. The negative or agnostic portion of their thought was absorbed by Spencer; while their qualified support of spiritualistic and religious belief was rapidly superseded by the rising influence of the Kantian and post-Kantian thought, for whose introduction into England Hamilton was himself partly responsible, and against which his polemic had been largely directed. This new and transforming influence had already permeated literature and popular thought through the medium of COLERIDGE and CARLYLE.[2] It now established itself in academic and scholarly circles through STIRLING'S[3] *Secret of Hegel*, which appeared in 1865, and marks the beginning of the idealistic movement which, through Caird, Green, Bradley, and oth-

---

[1] Hamilton was born in 1788, and died in 1856. His *Discussions on Philosophy and Literature* were published in 1852, and his *Lectures on Metaphysics* (posthumously) in 1859. Henry Longueville Mansel (1820–1871) is chiefly famous for his lectures on the *Limits of Religious Thought*, delivered and published in 1858.

[2] In particular through Coleridge's *Aids to Reflection*, published in 1825, in which the author invokes the Kantian conception of an intuitive "reason" to escape the metaphysical shortcomings of the "understanding." Samuel Taylor Coleridge was born in 1772 and died in 1834. Thomas Carlyle (1795–1881) was the great English apostle of romanticism, deriving his inspiration mainly from Fichte and Goethe. His *Sartor Resartus* appeared in 1833, his *French Revolution* in 1837, and in 1860 he was at work on his *History of Frederick II*.

[3] James Hutchinson Stirling, 1820–1909.

ers, came to dominate English philosophy at the close of the century.[1]

§ 5. America

AMERICA produced no eminent representatives of the naturalistic movement during the nineteenth century, but was influenced by contemporary English thought, as well as, to a lesser degree, by Comte. Mill was widely read, as Locke had been in the previous century, and his leadership was followed in circles of economic and political liberalism. Here, as in England, the scientific conception that most affected philosophical thinking was that of evolution.[2] The publication of Darwin's *Origin of Species* precipitated in America in 1860 a lively controversy both among scientists themselves and between the party of science and the party of religion. AGASSIZ, an eminent biologist and geologist, and a distinguished exponent of the spirit and method of science, resisted the Darwinian teachings, and defended both the immutability of species and the older hierarchical philosophy of nature.[3] The principal champion of Dar-

---

[1] § 17.

[2] The most eminent representative in America at this time of the new physics was Joseph HENRY (1797–1878). As Secretary of the Smithsonian Institution, and as first president of the National Academy of Sciences, founded in 1863, he accomplished much for the development of experimental science and of technology in America, but this movement appears to have exerted little or no influence in the direction of positivism or materialism. Josiah Willard GIBBS (1839–1903), one of the founders of physical chemistry, and perhaps the greatest of American scientists, was scarcely known outside the circle of his collaborators. The general standpoint of naturalism, especially in its opposition to religion, was represented by John William Draper (1811–1882) in his *History of the Intellectual Development of Europe* (1862) and his *Conflict between Religion and Science* (1874).

[3] Jean Louis Rodolphe Agassiz (1807–1873) had originally derived his zoölogical principles from Cuvier and his philosophy of nature from the

win was the botanist Asa GRAY.[1] These first American Darwinians did not find evolution to be in conflict with the traditional religious view of the world; but the teaching of Darwin, combined with that of Spencer, whose works were read in America almost as promptly and as widely as in England, exerted a powerful and growing influence in the direction of naturalism, and soon gave rise to an evolutionary philosophical cult, of which the most conspicuous leader was John FISKE.[2]

The academic philosophy of the time, providing a rational ground for the Protestant faith, was the Scottish realism, introduced in earlier days by WITHERSPOON, and now represented by McCOSH and PORTER.[3] This philosophy was not without a tincture of Kantianism, but the latter current came mainly, as in England, from two sources and in two successive waves. EMERSON[4] was at this time in the full vigor of his genius. While drawing inspiration from many sources, his "transcendentalism" was influenced largely by Coleridge's *Aids to Reflection*, and thus indirectly by Schelling. Like Coleridge and Carlyle in England, Emerson

---

teachings of Schelling. His chief disciple in America was Joseph Le Conte (1823–1901), whose *Evolution, Its Evidences and Its Relation to Religious Thought* appeared in 1891.

[1] 1810–1888; afterward supported by the geologist James Dwight Dana (1813–1895).

[2] 1842–1901. Fiske lectured on "The Positive Philosophy" in 1869; and published his *Outline of Cosmic Philosophy* in 1874.

[3] John Witherspoon (1723–1794) came from Scotland in 1768 to be president of the College of New Jersey (now Princeton University). James McCosh (1811–1894), a pupil of Hamilton, came from Scotland to the same institution just one hundred years later. Noah Porter (1811–1892) was president of Yale College from 1871 to 1886.

[4] Ralph Waldo Emerson, 1803–1882. *The Conduct of Life* appeared in 1860, the *Essays* having been published in 1842.

and the Transcendentalists represented post-Kantian thought in its romantic form and in its literary and popular manifestations. Transcendentalism was also linked with Scottish realism through the influence of Cousin, whose works were translated and widely read in the second quarter of the century. The second wave of Kantian influence came in America, as in England, in the form of the introduction of Hegel. The study and translation of this philosopher, inaugurated in 1867 by HARRIS,[1] marked the beginning in America of the idealistic movement, which numbered Howison and Royce among its more conspicuous leaders, and which rapidly rose to a position of ascendancy in the second half of the nineteenth century.[2]

[1] William Torrey Harris (1835–1909) founded in 1867 the *Journal of Speculative Philosophy* and was the leader of the so-called "St. Louis School." Owing to the influence upon Harris of a German pioneer named H. C. Brockmeyer, this movement may be said to have been in part a direct importation from Germany to the American Middle West.
[2] § 18.

PART II

NATURALISM, MATERIALISM, AND POSITIVISM

Just after the middle of the nineteenth century, naturalism, or the philosophy inspired by science, recovered an influence upon European thought similar to that which it had possessed at the close of the eighteenth century. But the new naturalism was governed by new motives. While the naturalism of the eighteenth century had been an effect of the mechanical theory, generalized by Newton, and now extended to life, mind, and society, the new naturalism was stimulated by the theories of evolution and conservation. The older naturalism had represented the cosmos as a system of moving bodies governed by mathematical law, while the newer naturalisms represented the cosmos as a majestic process of natural history, or as a fixed quantity of matter, force, or energy (substance) having multiple and variable manifestations. Along with these comprehensive materialistic views of the world, calculated, whatever the intent of their authors, to serve the purpose of a metaphysics, there arose the cult of positivism, which was concerned with the scientific way of thinking rather than with the scientific account of the world; or with science itself, rather than with nature. Considering naturalism first on its constructive side, as offering a complete picture of nature in terms of science, its most powerful impulse came from the biological conception of evolution.

§ 6. Darwin and Darwinism

CHARLES ROBERT DARWIN, born in 1809, was the grandson of Erasmus Darwin,[1] famous for his poetic versions of natural evolution and for his anticipation of the Lamarckian theory. The younger Darwin was graduated from Cambridge University, but owed his biological vocation less to his formal education than to his private studies and excursions as an amateur geologist; these culminating in his being chosen, in 1831, as naturalist to the expedition on board the *Beagle*. This expedition spent five years surveying the South American coasts and neighboring islands, and afforded Darwin abundant opportunity both to collect diverse forms of animal life and to observe their geographical distribution. Soon after his return he began his prolonged studies of the transmutation of species, leading to the publication in 1859 of his epoch-making work, *On the Origin of Species by Means of Natural Selection, or the Preservation of Favoured Races in the Struggle for Life*. This was followed by *The Variation of Animals and Plants Under Domestication*, in 1868; the *Descent of Man and Selection in Relation to Sex*, in 1871; and the *Expression of the Emotions*, in 1872. In spite of his frail health Darwin persevered in laborious and detailed studies of plant life up to within a few months of his death in 1882. His open-mindedness, scrupulousness, and union of inventive capacity with painstaking observation, together with the purity of his personal character, have

---

[1] 1731–1802.

NATURALISM AND POSITIVISM

justly led to his canonization among the patron saints of modern science.

Darwin made two major contributions to biology. In the first place, through his comprehensive survey of available data and his masterly inductions, he brought about the definitive scientific acceptance of the natural origin of new species of plants and animals. As a more or less speculative hypothesis, this view dated from the time of Empedocles in the fifth century before Christ. It had received the qualified indorsement of many eminent authorities, including Aristotle, Lucretius, St. Augustine, Bacon, Leibniz, Diderot, and Kant. In the century preceding Darwin's work this view had gathered force both from the speculations of philosophers of the romantic school, such as Herder, and from the observations of biologists such as Buffon.[1] The most notable of Darwin's scientific predecessors was Lamarck, who had not only adopted the general evolutionary point of view but also elaborated for its explanation a theory which has lately become the chief rival of Darwin's law of natural selection.[2] Even those biologists who believed in the immutability of species accepted a system of classification which called attention to the gradation of their differences, and there was much evidence to suggest that the lines between one species

---

[1] Johann Gottfried Herder (1744–1803); Georges Louis Leclerc, Count de Buffon (1707–1788).

[2] According to Lamarck's theory, organic changes develop through the activities which arise in response to the needs of life. Parts which are so exercised grow in the direction required for their functional use, and these acquisitions being inherited, become the starting-point for further developments in successive generations. Thus the race is continuously perfected by practice.

and another were arbitrarily drawn. The discovery of fossil remains indicated that some at least of the existing gaps which divide species are due to the extinction of earlier forms of life. Comparative anatomy and morphology brought to light unsuspected family resemblances among distinct species. Both paleontology and geography revealed a correspondence between forms of life and their physical environment. The new uniformitarian geology enormously extended the range of time in which new species might be supposed to be gradually developed upon the earth's surface. Above all, there was a steadily growing disposition on the part of biology to avoid appeal to supernatural or metaphysical causes, and to construe life as a part of that nature which is for scientific purposes a closed and self-sufficient system. All of these tendencies of thought converged in Darwin, and enabled him to secure the acceptance of a general view for which the times were ripe.

In the second place, Darwin formulated and verified a specific hypothesis for the explanation of the origin of species. To this hypothesis he gave the name of "natural selection."[1] The starting-point of the theory is the fact of *variation* among the individuals of the same species, or among the members of a generation sprung from the same ancestry. This is a familiar fact, of which the breeder takes advantage in the creation of a new stock. The causes of such "individual differences" are both numerous and obscure, and their discussion con-

---

[1] The following is a free rendering of the argument in *The Origin of Species*.

NATURALISM AND POSITIVISM   23

stitutes an important topic in itself; but these causes are not germane to the argument. For the breeder the important thing is that the differences occur, and that they afford him a wide range of choice. But animals and plants in a state of nature exhibit, albeit in a lesser degree, a like variability; and just as in the case of artificial selection some from among the many varieties will serve the breeder's purpose better than others, so in the state of nature some will better serve the needs of the organism itself. Just as the man who wishes to breed a stock of fleet greyhounds will find among his dogs some that are better built for speed than others, so among wolves who are forced by circumstances to prey upon deer there will be some who are relatively slimmer and swifter;[1] and as the former individuals are suited to the breeder's purpose, so the latter are suited to the circumstances of life, or *adapted to the environment*. We have now to ask whether there is any *natural* selective principle, analogous to the human breeder— one which guarantees that the better adapted animals shall survive and perpetuate their kind.

To understand this principle and its *modus operandi*, we have to recognize the prodigality of the reproductive process, which brings into existence many more individuals than the environment can sustain.[2] The effect of nature's excessive fecundity is to induce a competition for the limited available resources, or a "struggle

---

[1] *Op. cit.*, 1897, pp. 65–66.
[2] At this point both Darwin and his collaborator Wallace (§ 4) were indebted to the study by Malthus of the effects of overpopulation. Cf. Thomas Robert Malthus (1766–1834), *Essay on the Principle of Population* (1798).

for existence."[1] The majority must be eliminated: who, then, shall survive? The answer seems clear. Those who survive will be those, like the slimmer and swifter wolves, whose variations best adapt them to existing circumstances. Under severely competitive conditions even slight variations will be matters of life and death. There will be, to use Spencer's phrase, a "survival of the fit." In other words, elimination and survival will be selective, and will explain both the improvement of the stock and the peculiar correspondence between the organism and its habitat.

There is one final step to be taken, and the argument is complete. The "fit" who survive and grow to maturity will reproduce themselves, while the unfit will leave no issue. The second generation will inherit those favorable variations which enabled their parents to survive,[2] and will develop upon this level a new range of variations, among which the more favorable will again be selected by the same process; so that the effect will be cumulative, and will eventually lead to the formation of a new and relatively perfected[3] type. Thus the play of natural forces, by the addition of slight differences and without design, leads to the formation of organized structures that are progressively qualified to cope with the circumstances of life. By a sort of *coup*

[1] Wallace's phrase.
[2] Instead of inheriting the "acquired characteristics" of the parents, as in the Lamarckian and Spencerian theories, Darwinism, taken together with Weismann's theory of the "germ-plasm," rejects the inheritance of skill, strength, or habits that result from experience and exercise. Cf. below, § 7. The question is still disputed, with the preponderance of opinion on the side of Darwin and Weismann.
[3] Such adaptive perfection is always relative to the existing environment.

d'état those very aspects of life that had served the theory of intelligent design are now made to wear the livery of mechanism.

The theory of natural selection was proposed as the most important factor in evolution, rather than as a complete explanation. Its incompleteness was recognized by Darwin himself, and most of the objections since raised against it on this score were anticipated. In the first place, the theory assumed without explanation the fundamental vital processes, such as variation, growth, reproduction, heredity, and the self-preservative impulse which motivates the "struggle for existence." In the second place, the theory did not appear adequately to account for the survival of useless variations, or for such variations as are useful only when they have accumulated to the point sufficient to establish a new organ. It did not satisfactorily explain why the same variations arise simultaneously in individuals, as they must if they are not to be lost by cross-breeding. The biological criticism of Darwin has, therefore, taken the form of advancing other principles of selection, which supplement the Darwinian principle or reduce it to a place of secondary importance.[1]

Since Darwin was essentially a biologist, restrained from metaphysical speculation by the cautious temper of the scientist, how did it happen that his work should have created an epoch in philosophy as well as in science, and that he should have said, *apropos* of his con-

---

[1] Darwin himself introduced the principle of "sexual selection," or preferential mating, to account for useless variations; and the principle of "isolation" to explain the absence of interbreeding. Cf. *op. cit.*, ch. IV.

viction that species are not immutable, that it was "like confessing murder"?[1]

In the first place, the new theory violated prevailing habits of mind, rooted in the Aristotelian tradition and confirmed among biologists by the influence of Linnæus and Cuvier.[2] In accordance with these habits it was customary to *classify* the forms of life on the assumption that they had no history other than their reproduction in successive generations of individuals.

In the second place, the new view violated the teachings of biblical orthodoxy, or that account of natural origins which among devout Protestants was authoritatively recorded,—in prose in the Book of Genesis, and in poetry in Milton's *Paradise Lost*.

Deeper than either of these was the conflict between the new teaching and the teleological doctrines of the great philosophers. Both pagan and Christian philosophy had taught that nature could not be adequately explained without resort to a principle variously known as "purpose," "final cause," "Providence," and "design." The mechanical theory had made great inroads upon this doctrine and the living organism was looked upon as its last stronghold. If this marvel of nice adjustment and functional utility could be explained by the fortuitous operation of blind forces, then nature no longer afforded evidence of intelligence or of spirit or of God. Darwinism also created the impression of reducing nature to an all-pervading and ceaseless flux

---

[1] F. Darwin, *Life and Letters of Charles Darwin* (1887), vol. I, p. 384.
[2] Carolus Linnæus (1707–1778) and Georges Cuvier (1769–1832), founders respectively of systematic botany and comparative anatomy.

without refuge or anchorage. Life had always worn an aspect of generation and decay, but had been redeemed by the Platonic-Aristotelian idea that the forms which it embodied were permanent, and by the Christian idea that it was a manifestation of eternal benevolence. Now all of these moorings seemed to be dissolved into a flood sweeping blindly on without origin, destination, or fixed landmarks.

Finally, there was an obvious application to man which Darwin himself did not hesitate to make.[1] As one species among others, man, too, had his natural origin, and was conceived to spring from simian stock. There is a disposition to judge man's destiny by his source and to suppose that a lowly origin must contradict his high calling.[2]

Turning from these negative philosophical implications, we find in Darwin the germs of a more positive teaching concerning man and his place in the world. Darwin's studies of instinct and of emotional expression[3] were important and lasting contributions to the new science of psychology. His central conceptions are readily transposed to cognition, and have in recent times led to a theory of knowledge, in which concepts, like species, are regarded as plastic and variable, having a natural genesis and a capacity to survive according to the degree to which they fit the concrete situation to which they are applied.[4]

[1] In his *Descent of Man*.
[2] That Darwin himself did not accept such an inference, but regarded man's natural descent as an ennobling rather than degrading conception, appears in the closing paragraphs of his *Descent of Man*.
[3] *Origin of Species*, ch. VIII; *Expression of the Emotions*.
[4] Cf. E. Mach (§ 11) and J. Dewey (§ 25).

There were certain moral and religious implications which Darwin drew himself, or which his teachings suggested to others. What is, in the broad sense, known as "evolutionary ethics" assumed three quite distinct forms. Darwin proposed to reconcile evolution with traditional ethics through the conception of adaptation. Some degree of sociality, or of mutual aid and sympathy, is a condition of the survival of a race, and is therefore as "natural" as the self-seeking propensities. Conscience may be construed in this sense as a set of favorable variations. This is the form of evolutionary ethics which was further developed by Spencer. The second and third forms take the conception of struggle rather than that of adaptation, as their point of departure. According to the second view, developed by Huxley,[1] the natural life presents the antithesis of the moral life. In the natural life the individual exploits his superiority, and the weak are allowed to suffer the fatal consequences of their weakness; whereas in the moral life the weak are protected by the self-sacrifice or assistance of others. The third view would propose to accept capacity to survive as its criterion of good, and would reject the traditional ethics as interfering with the operation of the law of natural selection. Let the strong man assert his strength, and in this way guarantee the future of the race. It is this idea that links the teachings of Darwin with the ethics of Nietzsche.[2] The

---

[1] In his *Evolution and Ethics*.

[2] § 21. From the idea that the moral practice of civilized societies interferes with the law of natural selection and permits the weak to survive and reproduce themselves, has sprung the modern cult of *eugenics*. Cf. Karl Pearson, *Groundwork of Eugenics*, 1909.

extension of the same idea to social groups has been used by the Marxian socialists as a justification of classstruggle, and by extreme nationalists as a justification of war and aggrandizement.

As regards the religious implications of his teachings, Darwin was led more and more to the rejection of the traditional conception of a providential God. Not only did the law of natural selection, in his judgment, destroy the force of the argument from design, but it revealed nature in a light that was scarcely compatible with the supposition of benevolent authorship. Nevertheless his natural piety, together with his unwillingness to pronounce judgment on questions which he felt to lie beyond his competence and to involve the happiness of other people, deterred him from an aggressive *dis*belief. He wavered between a theistic belief in "laws impressed on matter by the Creator,"[1] and a tolerant and reticent "agnosticism."[2]

§ 7. Cosmic Evolution. Spencer

Darwin was the author of a scientific hypothesis which lent itself to philosophical interpretation and extension. HERBERT SPENCER, on the other hand, was a philosopher with a prepossession for science. With Darwin evolution was a biological law; with Spencer it was a cosmic generalization. He was born in Derby, England, in 1820. Declining the opportunity of a university education, he found employment from 1837, first as an engineer and afterward, until 1853, as subeditor of *The Economist*. By this time his central ideas

---

[1] *Origin of Species*, p. 402.   [2] *Life and Letters*, vol. I, ch. VIII.

were fixed and he was ready to devote the remainder of his life to their systematic elaboration. His scientific tastes and aptitudes inclined him from the beginning to the naturalistic philosophy. As early as 1839 he had derived the idea of development from a study of Lyell's *Geology*. In his *Social Statics*, published in 1850, he proposed to extend the idea of development to society. The first edition of his *Psychology*, published in 1855, revealed both his introduction of the same genetic method into the study of mind, and also his assimilation of the sensationalism and associationism of the British empirical tradition. In divers essays he had also made clear the strongly individualistic bias of his moral and economic thought. In 1857 a treatise on *Progress: Its Laws and Cause* set forth the general principle under which he proposed to subsume the totality of knowledge; and in 1860 he announced the plan of his *Synthetic Philosophy*, to be executed in ten volumes. To the fulfilment of this programme he devoted himself unrelentingly, despite the uncertainty of his health, for thirty-six years.[1] He died in 1902, a monument of methodical industry and heroic perseverance.

Spencer represents all of the different motives of the naturalistic school. Like Comte,[2] he found nature to culminate in society, and was one of the founders of

[1] The parts of his system and the dates of their completion are as follows: *First Principles*, 1862; *Principles of Biology* (two volumes), 1864–1867; *Principles of Psychology* (second edition, two volumes), 1870–1872; *Principles of Sociology* (three volumes), 1876–1896; *Principles of Ethics* (two volumes), 1879–1892. Among the more important of his smaller works are *Education* (1861) and *The Man versus The State* (1884). In addition he wrote many articles and pamphlets and an *Autobiography*, published in 1904.

[2] §§ 3, 9.

the science of sociology; and like Büchner and Haeckel,[1] he was profoundly influenced by the theory of the conservation of energy. But the most notable features of his thought are his limitation of knowledge to the field of experience and to the content of science; and his elaboration of a cosmic philosophy in terms of a generalization of the idea of evolution. Spencer's system thus falls into two main divisions, which are very unequally represented in his written works: his agnostic realism, defended in parts of the *First Principles* and *Psychology*, and his evolutionary survey of nature and man. The former constitutes the definition of his fundamental philosophical position and its reconciliation to the claims both of faith and of reason; the latter, his résumé and unification of the content of science.

With Hamilton and Mansel, Spencer subscribed to the doctrine of the "relativity of knowledge," and the consequent impossibility of knowing that non-relative or Absolute which has been the dream of metaphysicians.[2] To know a thing is to relate it to other things and to ourselves, or to introduce qualifying conditions; what the thing is unconditionally, must, therefore, escape us. But it does not follow, as Hamilton had supposed, that the unconditioned plays a wholly negative part in our thought. In the very recognition of our limits we refer beyond them to that Force which thrusts phenomena upon us. In calling it the Unknowable, therefore, Spencer did not imply doubt as to its existence. In fact, the Unknowable is in a sense the most familiar of objects. Science, in reaching out toward a

[1] §§ 1, 8.   [2] *First Principles*, part I.

first cause, or a final goal, or a supreme generalization, is perpetually forced to acknowledge it; the religious of all the ages have stood awe-struck in its presence. It thus furnishes the bond and the means of reconciliation between science and religion. Since the Unknowable cannot be known, science will of necessity relegate it to religion; but since science affirms the Unknowable, religion may be said to enjoy scientific support.

Over and above the dialectical proof of the Unknowable, there is a more empirical proof, derived from the examination of the data of experience. After the manner of Locke and Hume, Spencer distinguished between the relatively "vivid," constant, and uncontrollable impressions of sense, and the relatively "faint" and controllable series of ideas;[1] and in a manner that is reminiscent of Reid and Hamilton, he regarded the former as accompanied by a necessary belief in their externality of origin. This necessity of belief, or inconceivability of the opposite, thinks Spencer, is that which must always govern thought in the end. To affirm that of which the opposite is inconceivable is the "Universal Postulate" of cognition, or the ultimate test of validity.[2] Certainty diminishes, however, in proportion to the number of times that this test is employed. Judged by this criterion of relative certainty, the affirmation of external reality which accompanies sensations is more certain than an affirmation regarding these sensations themselves, since the latter presupposes the former. Idealism, which employs this derived or secondary cog-

[1] *First Principles*, part II, ch. II; *Principles of Psychology*, part VII, ch. XVI.
[2] *Principles of Psychology*, part VII, ch. XI.

nition, is therefore less certain than realism, which trusts the primary cognition of sensation. In other words, we are more certain (through perception) that there is an external reality than (through reflection) that we have perceptions of it.

Our "vivid" experiences give us knowledge of an external world through a sense of resistance, which is most unmistakable in the case of muscular sensation. We are thus led to represent the external reality to ourselves as a sort of power, acting on us in a manner analogous to that in which we act on ourselves, as when, for example, we press one hand upon another. But this representation is purely symbolic. Strictly speaking, all that we know of external reality through sensation is that there is a *something* which is thus manifesting itself to us—a something whose existence is undeniable but whose nature is unknowable.

The view of the Unknowable reached by this empirical approach Spencer calls "transfigured realism," as distinguished both from naïve realism and from idealism or scepticism.[1] It differs from naïve realism in that it denies that our sensations *reveal*, either in their content or in their order, the nature of objective fact. It differs from idealism, on the other hand, in affirming that the order of our sensations varies with objective fact, and is at all points determined by it, as the projection of a cube on the surface of a cylinder, although not cubical, is nevertheless so related to the cube that any changes in the latter will induce corresponding changes in the former.

[1] *Principles of Psychology*, §§ 472–474.

What is or is not inconceivable to us depends on certain established connections among our ideas, and therefore reflects the constitution of our minds. So much in general terms Spencer conceded to Kant. But as an associationist Spencer contended that this order among our ideas is an effect of the persistence or frequency of the vivid connections. The more often we experience things together, the more impossible it is for us to think them apart. To every new experience we thus bring certain habits of thought that reflect the experiences of the past, and that constitute our preformed and ingrained intelligence. This reflects not only the past experience of the individual, but ancestral experience as well, and may therefore be regarded, relatively to the individual, as *a priori*.[1] But it is justified because in its ultimate origin, or relatively to the racial experience, it is *a posteriori*, being a correspondence of internal to external relations. This was Spencer's proposed reconciliation of Kantian transcendentalism with British empiricism.

While Spencer's philosophy will be judged by critical historians in terms of its theory of knowledge, the powerful influence which it exerted in the latter half of the nineteenth century was due rather to its grandiose architecture than to the solidity of its foundations. In English-speaking countries it stood for several decades as the most imposing monument of science, in which the extensive but scattered results of research were so conjoined as to afford a unified picture of the total cosmos. The materials were drawn from all the special sciences, inorganic as well as organic, but they received

---

[1] *Principles of Psychology*, § 208.

NATURALISM AND POSITIVISM

their structural and pictorial unity from the principle of development or evolution. The conservation of energy, or, as Spencer preferred to call it, "the persistence of force,"[1] was accepted as the universal law governing physical changes, and defended on *a priori* as well as on experimental grounds. But this law applies to life and mind only when these are first reduced to physico-chemical terms. The only "synthetic" law which is directly applicable to phenomena of every level—which unites them all concretely, and which reveals their historical trend—is the law of increasing organization, or of correlative differentiation and unification. "Evolution is an integration of matter and concomitant dissipation of motion; during which the matter passes from an indefinite incoherent homogeneity to a definite coherent heterogeneity; and during which the retained motion undergoes a parallel transformation."[2] This principle Spencer both illustrated from existing science and extended into new fields. He found it in the evolution of the sidereal universe out of the primitive nebula; in the history and development of the earth; in the origin of life and of new and more complex species of organism; in the formation of complex ideas out of the primitive manifold of sensory "shocks"; in the building of an integrated will out of elementary reflexes; and in the progressive complication and organization of society. The application of this principle thus served the double purpose of exhibiting the fruitfulness of the genetic method, and of presenting nature as a totality

---

[1] *First Principles*, part II, ch. VII.
[2] *Ibid.*, part II, ch. XVII.

§ 8. Monism of Substance. Haeckel

ERNST HAECKEL, who was born in 1834, and died in 1919, and who was professor of zoölogy at the University of Jena from 1862, represents, like Spencer, the philosophical generalization of the content of science. He was the most influential exponent of naturalism in Germany during the last decades of the nineteenth century, his popularity culminating in the extraordinary vogue of his *Riddle of the Universe* (*Die Welträtsel*), first published in 1899.[1]

Like Spencer, Haeckel made philosophical use of the two great scientific theories of his age, the evolution of life and the conservation of energy. But while in Spencer the emphasis is placed on the former, in Haeckel it is placed on the latter; the cosmos being conceived, after the manner of Moleschott, Büchner, and other materialists of the German school,[2] as a constant quantity of dynamic substance underlying the variety of phenomenal manifestations. Unlike Spencer, Haeckel was a biologist of note,[3] and in promulgating his views he spoke as one having scientific authority. Being less philosophically disciplined than Spencer, he dealt more lightly with the traditional philosophical difficulties, and in particular with the problem of knowledge. He professed to be primarily interested in dispelling the super-

---

[1] His most important writings, in addition to the above, were his *Generelle Morphologie* (1866), *Natürliche Schöpfungsgeschichte* (1868), and *Anthropogenie* (1874). The *Schöpfungsgeschichte* has been translated into English under the title of *The History of Creation* (1883), and the *Anthropogenie* under the titles of *The Evolution of Man* (1879) and *The Pedigree of Man* (1880).

[2] § 1.   [3] An orthodox Darwinian.

NATURALISM AND POSITIVISM 39

stitions of the traditional religion and metaphysics, and in proclaiming a sort of new enlightenment, in which morality, government, education, and religion should profit by the recent extraordinary advance in physical science and technology. But his enthusiasm and dogmatic temper carried him far beyond the limits of this purpose, and led him to formulate a new metaphysics, which, whatever its truth, is certainly not less metaphysical than the old.

According to Haeckel, we know external nature through sense-impressions, and through "presentations" of which "we are convinced that their content corresponds to the knowable aspect of things." "We do not know 'the thing in itself' that lies behind these knowable phenomena," nor do we even "clearly know whether it exists or not." He left "the fruitless brooding over this ideal phantom to the 'pure metaphysician,'" and turned eagerly to his "monistic philosophy of nature." [1] He was not troubled, as was Spencer, by the fact that the very conceptions of "phenomena" and "correspondence" have ulterior implications, or by the fact that his philosophy of nature itself transcends both phenomena and the experimental results of science.

Nor was Haeckel seriously disturbed by the outstanding problems of science itself. In addresses delivered in 1872 in Leipzig and in 1880 before the Berlin Academy of Science, the physiologist Emil DUBOIS REYMOND[2] had pronounced his famous "Ignorabimus!"

---

[1] *Riddle of the Universe*, pp. 292, 380–381. References are to the English translation by J. M. McCabe, 1902.

[2] 1818–1896: *Ueber die Grenzen des Naturerkennens* (1872); *Die sieben Welträtsel* (1882).

We do not as yet, thought this cautious scientist, know the origin of life, the explanation of the orderly arrangement of nature, the origin of reason and of speech, or the truth about the freedom of the will; while on certain points, namely, the nature of matter and force, the origin of motion, and the origin of consciousness, we shall always remain in ignorance. But Haeckel had solutions of all these "seven riddles" in terms of two fundamental[1] laws.

Of these two great solvents the first was "the law of substance"—"the fundamental law of the constancy of matter and force." Although experimentally demonstrated by science, this law is, "in the ultimate analysis," "a necessary consequence of the principle of causality."[2] The constancy of matter and of force are basally the same thing, because matter and force are two aspects of the same substance, the one its space-filling or extensional aspect, the other its energetic aspect. Under the material aspect may be brought all corporeal forms, ponderable mass and imponderable ether, the first being only a condensation of the second, and the two occupying "infinite space" continuously; under the energetic aspect may be brought not only every variety of inorganic force, but the vital, psychic, and conscious "affinities" as well.

The second great solvent is "the universal law of evolution," by which life emerges from physico-chemical conditions, "psychoplasm" from protoplasm, and "neuroplasm" from psychoplasm. Life is the energetic

---

[1] *Riddle of the Universe*, pp. 15–16.
[2] *Ibid.*, pp. 381, 215.

aspect of protoplasm, unconscious mind of psychoplasm, and consciousness of the associative centres of the brain. Both cognition and will rise in brute and man through a series of "psychic gradations," from irritability and reflex action to conscious thought and purpose. All is one and continuous, and one can read either from above down, and endow the atom with a soul, or from below up, and declare that the mind is nothing but force.

The "monism of the cosmos," which is established on these two basic principles, of substance and of evolution, "proclaims the absolute dominion of 'the great eternal iron laws' throughout the universe. It thus shatters, at the same time, the three central dogmas of the dualistic philosophy—the personality of God, the immortality of the soul, and the freedom of the will."[1] The emancipated mind will worship Nature itself, or "the Goddess of truth" that "dwells in the temple of nature."[2] With this new "natural religion," which Haeckel proclaimed in opposition to the other-worldliness and asceticism of Christianity, was allied a new æsthetic cult inspired by the wealth of natural forms which modern science has disclosed to the human eye; a new education, based on the teaching of science; and the new "monistic ethics," credited to Herbert Spencer, in which egoism and altruism are reconciled through the development of the social instincts in successive generations of the race.

In two respects the materialistic naturalism which has just been expounded shows a tendency to pass over

[1] *Riddle of the Universe*, p. 381.   [2] *Ibid.*, p. 337.

into its philosophical opposite—in its emphasis on force, and in its emphasis on life.

Spencer believed the experience of force to afford the most adequate possible representation of the unknowable reality. Haeckel, like Büchner before him, while preserving the conception of matter, regarded force as its inseparable attribute. A step further in this direction was later taken by OSTWALD,[1] a prominent exponent of "energetics" both in physics and chemistry and in the philosophy of nature. This philosopher defines ponderable or tangible matter as a collocation of energies, its form being construed in terms of elasticity, its volume in terms of compressibility, and its mass in terms of work and velocity. Heat, electricity, sound, and light are readily subsumed under the same concept. Life itself is a peculiar combination of physico-chemical energies. Nature having been reduced to energy, the antithesis of body and mind disappears, for what is mind but energy? Instead of regarding psychical energy as parallel to physical energy, Ostwald proposes the bold hypothesis that it is convertible from and into physico-chemical energies through the intermediate form of nervous energy, in accordance with the law of conservation.[2] Thus energy becomes the universal substance and its constancy the universal law. But if physical energy and felt energy are thus interchangeable, it is as true to say that body has been reduced to

---

[1] Wilhelm Ostwald (1853–   ). The systematic presentation of his views is to be found in his *Vorlesungen über Naturphilosophie* (1902). Ostwald also approaches closely to the position of Mach (§ 11), both in his conception of an experience prior to the distinction of subject and object, and in his use of the norm of "economy" in scientific method.

[2] *Vorlesungen*, pp. 337 ff.

NATURALISM AND POSITIVISM

mind, as to say that mind has been reduced to body. From a naturalism of this type it is not difficult to find a way across to the spiritualism of Hartmann and Fechner.[1]

A bridge from materialistic naturalism to spiritualism and idealism is afforded also by its biological emphasis. Darwin, as we have seen, presupposed the fundamental vital processes, such as growth, reproduction, heredity, and organicity; and his influence tended to give vogue to these conceptions, and to biological ways of thinking. Furthermore, his own theory of natural selection seemed, through the conception of "struggle for existence," to justify the assumption of a sort of life-force, which in turn readily lent itself to a vitalistic and spiritualistic interpretation.

§ 9. The Rise of Positivism. Comte

Positivism is the critical rather than the metaphysical or materialistic form of naturalism. It adopts the scientific method and theory of knowledge, rather than its content and specific doctrines. Underlying this difference among types of naturalistic philosophy, there is a difference of attitude on the part of the scientist toward his own concepts—the difference, namely, between the scientific realist and the scientific nominalist. This difference is compatible with entire agreement in scientific doctrine. Of two scientists both may accept the same theory, such, for example, as the atomic theory; but one may believe nature really to consist of atoms hidden from human observation, while the other believes them to be convenient terms of dis-

[1] § 14.

course by which to describe the observable facts. A scientist of the first type is accustomed to think of the realities as lying beyond experience; and when he philosophizes he will, like Spencer and Haeckel, fall easily into the ways of metaphysics. The scientist of the second type carries with him into philosophy his characteristic partiality for the observable fact. He may allude to an unknown reality, but if so it will be to disavow his knowledge of it rather than to affirm its reality. From this cast of mind springs positivism, which affirms that for philosophy as for science the only reality that can be in question is the content of experience. To know is not to affirm an ulterior and hidden substance or power, but to frame laws which fit experience. Although the difference is one of degree rather than of kind, we may further distinguish the *empirical* positivists like Comte and Mill, who proclaim the standpoint of experience, and regard the descriptive law as a reproduction of the constant connections among observed facts; and the *economical* positivists like Lange, Mach, and Poincaré, who emphasize the factor of technic which is introduced into the situation by the scientist himself, and who hold that the laws of nature are in some degree constructed in accordance with the constitution, needs, or taste of the human mind.

Although he represents both varieties of positivism, together with the sociological tendency which culminates in Durkheim,[1] AUGUSTE COMTE may be regarded not only as the father of positivism in general, but as one who especially stressed its empirical motive.

[1] § 12.

NATURALISM AND POSITIVISM

Comte was born at Montpellier in 1789. He was identified as student, tutor, and examiner with the *École Polytechnique*, which under the Restoration continued the scientific traditions of the eighteenth century. His *Cours de Philosophie positive*,[1] containing his defense of the positive method and his famous *three stages*, placed him at once in the first rank of the thinkers of his time. Having from his earliest years a strong humanitarian and reforming impulse, and being an intimate associate of Saint-Simon,[2] he sought to find in positivism the basis for a social reconstruction which should serve as a safeguard against the disintegrating tendencies of revolution. This phase of his development culminated in the *Politique positive* (1851-1854), in which he introduced the "religion of humanity." In his last years he devoted himself with piety and zeal to the development of this new cult, which strongly colored both his thought and his personal life.[3]

Comte is to be understood as a sequel both to the French Revolution and to the scientific movement of the seventeenth and eighteenth centuries. Like all French philosophers of the Napoleonic and Restoration era, he was moved by a desire to reconstruct social in-

[1] Six vols., Paris, 1830-1842; 2d ed., with a *Preface* by Littré, 1864; English trans. by Harriet Martineau, 1853. Later writings: *Discours sur l'Esprit positive*, 1844; *Système de Politique positive*, 4 vols., 1851-1854 (English trans., 1875-1877); *Catéchisme positiviste*, 1853 (English trans., 1858).

[2] Cf. § 3.

[3] This cult was organized in England under the leadership of Frederic Harrison (1831-1923). Among those more or less closely associated with Comte and his influence were J. S. Mill (§ 10), E. Littré (§ 3), Taine, Renan, Cournot (§ 3), and S. Germain (1776-1831: *Considérations générales sur l'État des Sciences et des Lettres aux differentes Époques de leur Culture*, 1833).

stitutions upon a rational and stable basis. He believed that a coherent society could be established only through the general adoption of a coherent system of ideas, and by the unifying and invigorating influence of a common ideal. But that which had been achieved in the thirteenth century by the Catholic faith, could in the nineteenth century be achieved only by a new faith that should express the enlightenment of a new age. Hence the importance in Comte's philosophy of his famous law of the three stages (*les trois états*), by which the human mind progressively reaches maturity. These three stages are respectively: the theological or fictive, the metaphysical or abstract, and the scientific or *positive;* the last being the culminating stage at which mankind is at length emerging, and which must henceforth afford the only acceptable and secure foundation for civilization and its institutions.[1]

The theological stage is that in which man explains nature in terms of fictitious supernatural agencies modelled upon that kind of causation with which he is most familiar, namely, that exerted by his own conscious will. As the anthropomorphic way of thinking, it is primitive and spontaneous, affording a necessary first step to be improved upon later. Its highest achievement is monotheism, which reflects the steadily growing belief in the unity of nature. Metaphysics represents a transitional phase of thought. The mind is still impelled to explain phenomena in terms of beings and agencies behind the scenes, but in the light of increased scientific knowledge these can no longer be conceived

[1] *Positive Philosophy*, trans. by H. Martineau, 1893, I, 2.

as operating capriciously or providentially. Natural phenomena evidently have fixed properties and regular effects. The earlier theological beings are thus reduced to substances possessing these properties, and the earlier theological causes to forces generating these effects. They become mere abstractions, or hypostatizations of their empirical manifestations. As empty and superfluous, these metaphysical conceptions then disappear, leaving only the empirical manifestations, together with their constant properties and effects, as these are expressed in scientific laws.

In its scientific or positive stage science is essentially descriptive rather than explanatory. As regards content, it limits itself to the data of experience and must always appeal to these for its verification. As regards form, it seeks to conceive particular facts as varieties of more general facts, and to seize upon the relations of similarity and succession by which particular facts may be predicted. These relations are discovered by observation and induction, but once discovered they permit of the extension of knowledge to further particulars by deduction; so that *a posteriori* knowledge paves the way for *a priori* knowledge, and theoretical science for technology and control. While science affirms that nature is governed by invariable laws, this generalization is not assumed or proved in advance, but progressively verified, as the laws are actually found.[1] Scientific knowledge is "relative" in a double sense. The data of experience are conditioned by the constitution

---

[1] Comte here agrees with Mill. Cf. Comte's *Discours sur l'Esprit positif*, and below, § 10.

48 PHILOSOPHY OF THE RECENT PAST

of human nature, while the categories and methods employed in science are conditioned by the general cultural *milieu*, and by the stage of evolution at which society has arrived.

Next in importance after his law of the three stages is Comte's classification of the sciences. He recognized six fundamental (theoretical, abstract) sciences, each of which arrives at distinct and irreducible laws of its own: mathematics, astronomy, physics, chemistry, biology, and sociology. There are several principles which determine this order of arrangement. In the first place, the objects of each in turn are more *complex* and concrete than those of their predecessors. Thus while mathematics deals with nature, it deals only with its most simple and abstract characters; while sociology, at the other extreme, deals with humanity, which is the most complex and concrete of all existences. In the second place, each science in turn *depends* on its predecessors, physics employing the laws of mathematics, biology the laws of physics and chemistry, and sociology the laws of all. This does not mean that sociology is reducible to mathematics, but is founded on it; mathematics being true of humanity, but only very inadequately true. Nature is continuous and self-consistent, its several laws forming harmonious parts of one encyclopædic system; but at the same time it is to be conceived as rising successively to different levels where new laws obtain.[1]

Thirdly, Comte's classification of the sciences repre-

---

[1] Comte may be said thus to have anticipated the contemporary conception of "emergence." Cf. below, §§ 13, 30.

NATURALISM AND POSITIVISM 49

sents the order in which these have achieved the "positive" method. Mathematics was the first science to be a true science, and has almost wholly escaped the taint of theology and metaphysics. Sociology is the last of the sciences to mature. Up to Comte's own time it had been assumed that, whatever might be the case with other parts of the known world, humanity, at least, was inaccessible to the scientific method. Thus Comte prided himself not only on having raised the banner of the positive method, but on having been himself responsible for the last and most glorious of its conquests. For, in bringing humanity within its rule, positivism annexes at one stroke the whole family of philosophical disciplines, such as logic, ethics, æsthetics, and religion; and thus, by achieving a universal dominion, becomes itself a philosophy. Finally, as the sciences mount in the scale of complexity, their subject-matter loses that aspect of fatality which attaches peculiarly to mathematics. Phenomena such as life and society are relatively unpredictable owing to their complexity, and are relatively subject to human control owing to the large number of causes which are operative. Thus society is *par excellence* the field for the exercise of the will.[1]

Comte's philosophy both centres and culminates in sociology. It is in terms of sociology that the traditional

---

[1] The most notable omission in Comte's classification of the sciences is psychology. This omission is due to his profound distrust of the introspective method, as abused by his contemporaries the "idealogues" (cf. above, § 3, and below, § 15); and to its incompatibility with the methods of the other sciences. He believed that whatever was genuinely scientific in psychology could be divided between biology and sociology. Cf., *e. g.*, *Cours de Philosophie positif*, 1869, III, pp. 530–589. His view may be compared with the contemporary view known as "behaviorism" (cf. below, § 29).

philosophical inquiries are to be given a scientific form. Thus a scientific logic is that which describes the modes of thought which have actually been practised by mankind in the several stages of its evolution; while a scientific ethics will describe the social conditions which have given rise to the several moral and political codes, and will examine the relations which bind the individual to the group, and the method by which, in the light of history, these relations may be cultivated. The innermost of all philosophical problems, that of knowledge itself, is not to be treated by the method of reflection and analysis, but by an empirical study of the history of knowledge, science being viewed as an institution or social activity. Sociology is thus not only the last of the sciences, but it is the science of the sciences. It provides the only possible centre by which nature may be rounded into a unified whole. Viewed as a manifold of objects, nature is boundless and incomplete; viewed as a system of sciences, it may all be seen as an expression of organized humanity.

Comte's philosophy is socio-centric not only in its theory of knowledge, but in its goal of aspiration and object of worship. Man finds his highest vocation in his participation in a continuous and unified humanity, which is the most complex and noble, as well as the most imperfect and dependent, of beings. The individual is united to society not by unconscious physical bonds but by his free intelligence and moral will. It is a unity of co-operation rather than of constraint. Humanity as the Great Being—the personification of the highest possibilities of human nature, is the proper object of adoration. Its heroes and benefactors are the objects of a grateful commemoration which both ennobles the living and immortalizes the dead.

Although Comte's original position is empirical and realistic, it is clear that there are motives in his thought which tend in a different direction, toward an economical positivism, and even toward idealism. Science at any given time is itself a historic and social product which reflects the existing stage of human development. Thus in the last analysis science will be what man makes it. Comte's originality lay in his substituting society for the individual knower, or for an abstract epistemological subject, but there is none the less an ineradicable subjectivity in science. The Kantian solution of the problem was to withdraw this subjectivity altogether from nature, and give it an *a priori* and "transcendental" status. Rejecting this alternative, Comte could not escape the difficulty of making, at one and the same time, science the product of nature, and nature the product of science. There remain for him, as for all non-Kantians, only two alternatives. Either one must construe the advance of scientific enlightenment, the development of its categories and technic, as the progressive self-revelation of a pre-existing natural order; or one must suppose that nature develops *pari passu* with science, thus constituting a progressive realization of man. Although the general bias of Comte's philosophy favors the former alternative, he tended unmistakably in his later years to the latter. Science is an instrument of the will, and the will is governed by love. Mankind, which is the proper object of worship, is also the key to the understanding of the world; and the logic of the heart takes precedence of the logic of the mind.[1]

§ 10. Empirical Positivism. Mill

JOHN STUART MILL[2] became interested in Comte when his own general philosophical attitude was already fixed, and in his work on *Auguste Comte and Positivism*, published in 1865, he acknowledged him as an ally rather than as a master. With the Comte of the *Positive Philosophy* he found himself in fundamental agreement, while he deemed this author's "subsequent speculations false and misleading."[3] To Mill the essential truth of Comte lay in his limitation of knowledge to the succession and similitude of phenomena, his three stages of intellectual development, his classification of the sciences, and his provision for a science of society. Mill differed broadly from Comte in being less systematic, and both more logical and more psychological. This was due in part to the fact that he was an Englishman, and in part to his education and philosophical sources. As an Englishman he was suspicious of speculation, and his relations with the British empirical school inclined him to analyze the data of experience rather than to trace the history of nature or of society.

---

[1] *Politique positif*, I, 447; II, 101–102.
[2] His principal works, other than those mentioned in the text, were the *Principles of Political Economy*, 1848; *Essay on Liberty*, 1859; *Considerations on Representative Government*, 1860; and the *Autobiography*, 1873.
[3] Edition of 1907, p. 5. Mill first became acquainted with Comte's philosophy in 1837; cf. *Autobiography*, 1873, pp. 207–213.

NATURALISM AND POSITIVISM

Similarly, as a philosophical technician, he was more interested in the proof of scientific knowledge than in the classification of the sciences.

Born in London in 1806, and being the son of James Mill, he was reared in the tradition of the introspective associationist psychology, of which his father was an eminent representative. His early studies of logic brought him to see the importance of the problem of *induction;* and his profound and original study of this problem resulted in the publication, in 1843, of his *System of Logic*,[1] generally regarded as the greatest of his works. The *Logic* is the application of empiricism to the method of science. In his *Examination of the Philosophy of Sir William Hamilton* (1865) Mill examined the other outstanding problem of empiricism, namely, that of the relation between perception and the external world.

Meanwhile, Mill's ethical, economic, and political views had been developing, first under the influence of the utilitarian school, of which he was a hereditary member. The founder of this school was JEREMY BENTHAM,[2] and James Mill was his most authoritative successor. This influence was, however, crossed and modi-

---

[1] This work underwent much revision in successive editions, of which the most important were those of 1850 and 1872. Mill acknowledged his indebtedness, as regards his logic and philosophy of science, not only to Comte, but to William Whewell (1794–1866), whose *History of the Inductive Sciences* appeared in 1837; and to Sir John F. W. Herschel (1792–1871), whose *Discourse on the Study of Natural Philosophy* had appeared in 1830.

[2] 1748–1832. His most important work was his *Introduction to the Principles of Morals and Legislation*, published in 1789. The doctrines of this school can be traced to Hume and to Richard Cumberland (1631–1718).

fied by two others. On the one hand, Mill was brought by a reaction against his early education, and by the cultural and romantic movement led by Coleridge and Carlyle,[1] to recognize the insufficiency of a purely quantitative and individualistic theory of value. On the other hand, he was led by his studies of political economy[2] to believe that the condition of the individual could be bettered only by a profound reconstruction of the foundations of society. Thus despite his individualism he was attracted to the programme of socialism. The fundamental principles of his ethics were set forth in his essay on *Utilitarianism*, published in 1863. His practical philosophy, in all the stages of its development, was influenced by his active participation in affairs. Appointed to the East India Company in his youth, later a clerk and examiner in the India House, and afterward a member of Parliament, he was trained to think concretely, and to translate theory into terms of practice. His views on religion, which were partially developed in his studies of Comte and Hamilton, were summarily but fragmentarily expressed in the three essays on *Nature, The Utility of Religion*, and *Theism*, published shortly after their author's death, which occurred in 1873. Mill was always more concerned with the truth as he saw it at the moment than with consistency or architectural unity; so that while his critics have found him shallow and incoherent, his admirers have found him to embody that candor and directness

---

[1] § 17.
[2] After Adam Smith (1723-1790) and David Ricardo (1772-1823), Mill was the most important founder of this modern science.

NATURALISM AND POSITIVISM

of attack which is peculiarly characteristic of the genius of British philosophy.

As an empiricist, Mill held that all knowledge appeals in the last analysis to the test of experience. Deductive thinking draws conclusions by inference from a major premise, but this major premise itself, such as "all men are mortal," is a universal statement of fact which must be obtained by induction. The fundamental topic of logic is therefore the question how such universal statements of fact can be justified. They appeal to the invariable connections found in experience, and the first step is to distinguish the connections that are "unconditional" from those that are due to the presence of ulterior circumstances. This distinction is facilitated by experiment, which can vary conditions *ad libitum;* and to perfect this procedure, Mill formulated his "four methods of experimental inquiry."[1] By the method of "agreement" we compare situations having only one common antecedent A, and if we then find only one common consequent a, we may say that a is related to A unconditionally, that is, independently of the other varying conditions. By the method of "difference" and its combination with the method of agreement, we compare situations in which a occurs with situations in which it fails to occur, and find that they differ only in that A is present in the one case and absent in the other. By the method of "residues" we eliminate the connections already known, and conclude that there is a connection between the A left over and the a not yet accounted for. Finally, by the method of

[1] *Logic*, book III, ch. VIII.

"concomitant variation" we conclude that there is a connection between A and a because for every change of A there is a corresponding change of a.

But there remains a more fundamental and a more difficult question. Suppose it to be proved by the four methods that A and a are unconditionally connected, both in experience and in experiment, does this justify the *generalization* of this connection? If there were a limited number of cases and one had exhausted all of them, then one's induction could be said to be complete. But the number of A's and a's is supposed to be unlimited. Am I justified because of their unconditional connection *thus far*, or within experience *up to date*, in concluding that they are connected always and everywhere? The fact is, says Mill, that our reasoning thus far has assumed the principle of "the uniformity of nature." The proof of this principle he believes that he discovers in its very generality.[1] Since it is presupposed as an underlying hypothesis in every particular hypothesis, the verification of every particular hypothesis adds evidence in its support. Inasmuch as all laws exemplify it, it cannot be overthrown, but must always be confirmed, by the discovery of any particular law; whereas one particular law may be overthrown by another. Furthermore, its universal claims add force to the fact that no breach of it has yet been detected. In other words, if it did not hold we should be peculiarly likely to know it.

Mill followed his predecessors of the empirical and nominalistic school in holding that our ideas are all re-

[1] *Logic*, book III, ch. XXI.

NATURALISM AND POSITIVISM 57

ducible to sensations, and that these are given to us severally, being united by association. The virtue of Mill's theory of knowledge lies in the persistence with which he attempted to reduce both the external world and the mind to these terms. The external world is an inference which is made by supposing that the relations, such as causality, which appear *among* sensations hold also between the total manifold of sensations and some realm lying beyond them. Such an inference is possible, but gratuitous. All that experience strictly verifies is the belief that, given certain sensations, others will follow. Matter, interpreted in terms of actual experience, means nothing but these constant uniformities, or these "permanent possibilities of sensation."[1] Mind is a set of possibilities of another order, differing in their arrangement, in their inclusion of thoughts, emotions, and volitions, as well as sensations, and in their being possibilities for one individual alone. But Mill recognized here the peculiar difficulty presented by the fact that the mind, although a series of states, can somehow grasp itself all at once as a unity. We must either give up the notion that the mind *is* a "series of feelings," or accept the doubtful view that a series can be aware of itself as a series. He thus bequeathed the problem of the unity of consciousness as an unsolved problem to his successors.[2]

In ethics, Mill, like Bentham, took his stand on the principle that actions are to be judged by their conse-

---

[1] *Examination of the Philosophy of Sir Wm. Hamilton*, ch. XI.
[2] *Ibid.*, ch. XII. Idealists, such as Green (§ 17), rejected the view that mind is a series, while radical empiricists, such as James (§ 25), retained the view and sought to explain the difficulty.

quences, and "are right in proportion as they tend to promote happiness, wrong as they tend to produce the reverse of happiness."[1] He also held, with Bentham, that the happiness by which the rightness of acts is to be judged is the general happiness, or happiness of the community, or greatest happiness of the greatest number. The proof of this principle, according to Mill, lies in the fact that each person desires his own happiness, so that, each person's happiness being a good to that person, the general happiness is "a good to the aggregate of all persons."[2]

Mill differed from Bentham in two important respects. In the first place, he greatly softened the latter's selfish and pleasure-seeking psychology. According to Mill, man comes, owing to his original sympathy and his acquired education, to desire virtue for its own sake. Instead of valuing it as a means to his pleasure, he values it for itself, and finds his pleasure *in* it. In the second place, he adds a qualitative to Bentham's purely quantitative scale of values. Some pleasures, and particularly those which involve reason and virtue, are "higher" pleasures, not because they are greater, in respect of intensity or duration, but because they are *preferred*.[3] Thus Mill sought to free utilitarianism from the odium which attached to it as a sordid and base philosophy that justifies the appetites and material comforts in opposition to the cultural and spiritual values.

In his practical ethics Mill was a strong champion of personal liberty. By allowing the individual to develop

[1] *Utilitarianism*, ch. I.   [2] *Ibid.*, ch. IV.   [3] *Ibid.*, ch. II.

freely in his own way, restricting him only as may be necessary in order to protect others, one both promotes the happiness of the individual himself and enriches the life of the community. Through his recognition of the higher pleasures, through his individualism, and through the provision made in his political philosophy for the representation of minority opinion, he hoped to save democracy from vulgarity and from the tyranny of the masses.

As against Hamilton and Mansel, he contended that the relativity of knowledge does not prove the inconceivability of God, but only the futility of conceiving God abstractly as the *Absolute* and *Infinite*. We cannot know anything except in its relations to ourselves, but it is as possible to know God relatively as it is to know nature relatively. He is especially vigorous in his rejection of Mansel's view that we must accept and worship a God whose nature violates both reason and conscience.[1] There is another alternative, which is to conceive God as finite, imputing to him only so much of the world as testifies to his goodness. Belief in a God who is the champion of righteousness gives to man a sense of partnership and reinforcement, and is thus morally fruitful, even though it be incapable of proof by the strict standards of the intellect. Religion, in the end, is an invigorating and comforting hope, rather than a reasoned conviction.[2]

[1] *Examination of the Philosophy of Sir Wm. Hamilton*, ch. VII.
[2] *Three Essays on Religion.*

§ 11. Economical Positivism. Lange. Mach. Poincaré

Empirical positivism may be termed "critical" in the sense that it limits knowledge to the field of experience. It is, on the other hand, deemed uncritical by those who believe that it ignores the part played in knowledge by the knowing mind. Empiricism is disposed to construe the subject as the passive recipient of sensations, and to interpret knowledge as reflecting an order which is *given* in experience. The knowing mind must frame hypotheses, but these are in the end tested and verified by their correspondence with experience; the knowing mind may even possess its ingrained modes of thought, but these are habits built up by association, and traceable to the routine of individual or ancestral experience. Economical positivism, on the other hand, denies the possibility of this reduction of knowledge to what is given, and insists that knowledge must always, even in the last resort, betray a bias of the knowing mind. The positivist of this type will, like all positivists, hold that natural science is the supreme example of knowledge, and will be interested in it *as knowledge* rather than as offering an account of the world we live in; but unlike the empirical positivist, he will be concerned with its subjective or formal factor—with that part of scientific knowledge which is supplied not by experience but by the scientific activity itself.

The German philosopher ALBERT LANGE,[1] professor at Zurich and Marburg, and author of the famous *History of Materialism* (*Geschichte des Materialismus*, 1866),

[1] 1828–1875 (§ 1).

NATURALISM AND POSITIVISM 61

serves through the very ambiguity and instability of his position, as the best starting-point for the study of this type of positivism. Being the source of diverging tendencies, he has been universally criticised by those who have followed some one of these tendencies to the exclusion of the rest. Lange took as his point of departure Kant's *Critique of Pure Reason*, which he believed to have proved once and for all that instead of our concepts being determined by objects, objects are determined by our concepts.[1] Our knowledge, in other words, reflects the organization of our minds. He also held, in accordance with the strict interpretation of Kant, that the categories or forms of mental organization apply only within the realm of experience; that the natural sciences afford the sole instance of their application, and hence the sole instance of knowledge; and that the only valid categories of science, and hence of knowledge, are those categories, such as space, time, and causality, which serve to provide an exact mechanical explanation of nature. While he thus supported the method of science, he denied the pretensions of a materialistic metaphysics, on the ground that, like all metaphysics, it illegitimately extends the categories beyond experience; and on the ground that it must necessarily fail in its attempt to reduce mind to physical terms.[2] So far he might, with justice, hold himself to be no more than a rigorous Kantian.

He clearly departed from Kant, however, in constru-

---

[1] *Geschichte des Materialismus*, 6th edition, II, 3.
[2] It can go no further in this direction than to establish a parallelism of aspects between the physical and mental (*op. cit.*, 2d edition, II, 374 ff.). Lange's view here approaches that of Fechner (§ 14).

ing the organization of the mind in *physico-psychological* terms, as a fact of human nature proved by such evidence as was in Lange's time supplied by the new physiology of the senses. Here the orthodox neo-Kantians[1] refused to follow him, contending that categories which are employed to construct our knowledge of nature cannot be a part of nature, but must be "transcendental," as Kant himself supposed them to be. Those who, like Lange, attempted to provide a naturalistic account of the categories definitely broke at this point with the Kantian tradition, and ceased to be affiliated with idealism.

The second part of Lange's philosophy was not less suggestive and prophetic than the first. Nature, or the world of knowledge, is common to all, expressing, as it does, the mental organization of the species. Over and above this realm of actuality there is the ideal realm, which is the free creation of the inventive or poetic imagination (*Dichtung*) of the individual.[2] When ideals are mistaken for actualities error arises, but ideals are the legitimate expression of the moral, æsthetic, and religious nature, and as such may be compared with one another in respect of their *value*. This view that the claims of ideals are to be judged by their own peculiar standards, independently of their reference to fact, relates Lange to Lotze and Ritschl,[3] and to the later development of the philosophy of value.[4] From this position it is but a short step to the view that truth itself is a value, and that even scientific judg-

[1] § 19. [2] *Op. cit.*, II, 540.
[3] § 14. [4] §§ 19, 28.

ments are justified, not solely by their conformity to outer fact, but by their satisfaction of the will. Here again there is a division between those philosophers who interpret the will naturalistically and are the forerunners of pragmatism,[1] and those philosophers who, adhering more closely to the Kantian teaching, interpret the will in transcendental and *a priori* terms.[2]

For the purpose of illustrating that widely diffused methodological positivism which rejected the Kantian deduction of the categories, but which nevertheless admitted a subjective or voluntary factor in knowledge, it will be most instructive to select two thinkers who approached philosophy through science.[3] This philosophy expressed the desire, on the one hand, to reduce the objects of science to the terms of experience, and, on the other hand, to reduce its categories to the actual technic of experimentation. It ought to avoid, on the one hand, speculative excursions beyond the given facts, and, on the other hand, logical schematisms and assumptions. It therefore represents the positivistic motive of science in its purity. But whereas the empirical positivists believed that the form of science, and hence the order of nature, reproduced the general features of experience, the members of the present group called attention to a selective factor in the scientific activity,

---

[1] §§ 22–25.   [2] § 20.

[3] Among the other scientists who exhibited the same general tendency of thought are the physicists Maxwell (§ 1), H. Hertz (1857–1894), G. Kirchhoff (1824–1887), and the physiologist M. Verworn (1863–1921). The most important of the philosophers affiliated with this tendency are Richard AVENARIUS (1843–1896; *Kritik der reinen Erfahrung*, 1888); his follower, J. Petzoldt (b. 1862); H. Cornelius (b. 1863); and Karl Pearson (b. 1853; *Grammar of Science*, 1892).

64 PHILOSOPHY OF THE RECENT PAST

which was accounted for in terms of the organism's need or taste for *economy*.

ERNST MACH, born in 1838, was for many years professor of physics at the University of Prague, and afterward, until his death in 1916, professor of philosophy in Vienna. His *Die Mechanik in ihrer Entwicklung*, published in 1883,[1] is a historical and critical study of scientific method, in which the author shows that in the course of its development mechanics has come more and more clearly to see that its purpose is "the abstract quantitative expression of facts." It does not seek to "explain" phenomena by referring them to purposes or hidden causes, but gives a simple and comprehensive account of the relations of dependence *among* phenomena.[2] His most notable philosophical work, the *Analysis of Sensations*, first published in 1886,[3] attacks the question of the relations of physics and psychology, reducing their content to common terms, and defining scientific method in such wise as to be applicable equally to both branches of investigation. Mach spoke as a scientist and disclaimed any intention of solving "riddles of the universe." He was only clearing the ground for science by eliminating problems with which the scientist is not concerned. But he clearly implied by the ironical tone in which he referred to "sure foun-

[1] Translated into English under the title of *The Science of Mechanics*, 1893.

[2] *Ibid.*, p. 502.

[3] *Beiträge zur Analyse der Empfindungen*. The 5th edition of 1906 contains important additions. Both editions have been translated into English under the title of *The Analysis of Sensation*. His other important philosophical works are *Populär-wissenschaftliche Vorlesungen*, 3d edition, 1903 (English trans., *Popular Scientific Essays*, 1910), and *Erkenntnis und Irrtum*, 1905.

dations" and "unshakable axioms," that what is good for the scientist is good also for the philosopher.[1]

Mach's boldest step was his resolution of body and mind into common elements. Here the way had been prepared for him by Berkeley, Hume, Mill, and others of the sensationalistic school, who had taught that physical things in their *knowable* aspect may be reduced to the sum of their sensible properties. Many of these philosophers had also proposed to reduce mind to a similar congeries of feelings. But, save for a suggestion of Hume,[2] these philosophers had regarded the members of both complexes as mental. The physical object still lurked behind the scenes as a duplicate of its sensible appearances, or as the activity of God, or as the Unknowable, or as a permanent possibility of sensation. Mach took the radical step of *identifying* the physical object with its sensible appearances. There is then no difference between the physical and the mental save the type of dependence among elements which in themselves are *neither* physical nor mental. The visible color, for example, is intrinsically neither physical nor mental; but in so far as dependent upon its luminous source it is physical, while in so far as dependent on the retina (as proved by its disappearance when the eyes are closed) it is mental. "Physical" and "mental," in other words, signify different *systems* of homogeneous elements.[3] An element's dependence on other elements within one or the other of these two systems is deter-

---

[1] *Erkenntnis und Irrtum*, Preface, and ch. I.
[2] *Treatise of Human Nature*, Selby-Bigge's edition, p. 207.
[3] *Analysis of Sensation*, English trans., 1914, pp. 8–17. The aggregate of these homogeneous elements in their bare qualitative differences constitutes the "pure experience" of Avenarius.

mined by the *method of variations*, or by the observation of the changes of one element which are correlated with changes observed or experimentally induced in other elements. When an element belongs to two systems, as when an element is both a sensation and the constituent of a body, the two sets of relations are distinguished by keeping the one set constant while varying the other.[1]

Mach was far from supposing that science is the mere observation or reproduction of the data of experience. Its purpose is to "save experiences," by achieving ideas in which these are summarized and anticipated.[2] It is governed by the purpose of *economy*. It is therefore primarily concerned not with the elements of experience, but with the "functional relations"[3] by which they are controlled. How far these functional relations, which appear as concepts and theories in the finished product of knowledge, subsist among the elements themselves, and how far they are the creation of science, is not clear. They are observed in phenomena, abstracted from phenomena, and verified by phenomena. On the other hand, they are tested subjectively by their congruence with one another, and possess a precision and a logical structure which is approximated but never fully realized in experience. Their very convenience as working tools is due to their being freely fashioned to the use to which they are put. In any case they owe their form to the necessity of *restricting expectation* to that which is vitally important. They are

---

[1] *Op. cit.*, pp. 344–345; *Erkenntnis und Irrthum*, ch. I.
[2] *Science of Mechanics*, pp. 481, 490.
[3] *Analysis of Sensation*, 1914, p. 363.

NATURALISM AND POSITIVISM 67

a "product of the *psychological* need of finding our way in nature," and their growing refinement expresses the demand for a more *methodical adaptation* that shall keep pace with the increasing complexities of life.[1]

The tendency of recent French philosophy of science has been to give greater emphasis to this subjective element which is recognized by Mach. The most important influence in this direction from the side of positivism was that exercised by the great mathematician and physicist HENRI POINCARÉ,[2] who at the opening of the century published a series of books dealing with the method and value of science.[3] He was born at Nancy in 1854, was a student and lecturer at the École Polytechnique in Paris—and afterward, from 1886 until his death in 1912, a professor of the Faculty of Sciences at the Sorbonne.

In addition to the fact that Poincaré was a creative scientist of great theoretical acumen, and qualified to speak with authority of scientific motives and scientific procedure, the interest of his philosophy lies in his attempt to combine three aspects of science—the rational, the conventional, and the experimental; each of which has had its partisans, but none of which in Poincaré's

---

[1] *Erkenntnis und Irrtum*, ch. XXIII.
[2] The tendency is further represented by Gaston Milhaud (1858–1918), *Essai sur les Conditions et les Limites de la Certitude logique* (1894), and Pierre Duhem (1861–1916), *La Théorie physique* (1906).
[3] These books, constituting only the philosophical part of his numerous publications, were *La Science et l'Hypothèse*, 1902 (English trans., *Science and Hypothesis*, 1914); *La Valeur de la Science*, 1905 (English trans., *The Value of Science*, 1907); *Science et Méthode*, 1909 (English trans., *Science and Method*, 1914); *Dernières Pensées*, posthumous.

judgment affords an adequate picture of science as a whole.

As a pure mathematician who is himself to be credited with important contributions to the theory of functions, Poincaré could scarcely fail to make a place in science for the element of universal and *a priori* truth. This he provided for in his account of "reasoning by recurrence,"[1] which he believed to lie at the basis of the simplest branch of mathematics, namely, arithmetic. That which is true of the number 1, and which when true of $n-1$ is true of n, is true of all numbers. This general theorem can be verified in the case of any given number by showing that if the truth in question holds of 1 it holds of 2, and if of 2, then of 3, and so on until the given number is reached. To establish the law for *all* numbers by this procedure would require an interminable and, therefore, psychologically impossible, series of syllogisms. The generalization of the law is possible only because the mind can see, once and for all, the possibility of this interminable series. We are forced to rely on a "direct intuition of the mind," which "knows itself capable of conceiving the indefinite repetition of the same act when once this act is possible."[2] From this intuition, and neither from the principle of contradiction nor from experience, is derived all generalization and universality.

When we pass from arithmetic and analysis, or the sciences of pure order, to geometry and to physics, the

---

[1] *La Science et l'Hypothèse*, part I, ch. I. This principle is sometimes known as "mathematical induction."

[2] *Science and Hypothesis*, English trans., 1905, p. 13.

principle of recurrence no longer suffices. There now appears the factor of *convention* or arbitrary definition. Poincaré was here influenced by the newer developments of mathematics, and in particular by non-Euclidean geometry.[1] The three-dimensional homogeneous space of Euclid and of common sense has ceased to possess any unique validity for mathematics, but is seen to rest upon certain assumptions which are, from the point of view of mathematics, quite arbitrary. By changing the assumptions mathematics can with equal validity develop a system of four-dimensional space. A similar range of possibilities exists in mechanics, in which the Newtonian system, for example, is only one alternative; or in mathematical physics, as exemplified by the theory of energy. In this field of free construction it is not strictly correct to speak of comparative truth. No one of these systems is *a priori* necessary, that is, derived solely and exclusively from the principle of recurrence, which they all employ in common. Nor do they owe any allegiance to the order of experience—which suggests them all, but does not dictate any one of them. They represent the free play of the scientific imagination, in which the mind, acting obediently to the principle of recurrence, is otherwise governed solely by æsthetic motives.

How, then, is one to choose among these alternatives? To find a criterion we must consider the relations of science to experience. Here enters the third, or empirical, aspect of science. Poincaré firmly opposed the ex-

---

[1] As developed by G. R. B. Riemann (1826–1866) and N. I. Lobatchewsky (1793–1856).

treme position of those who hold that science as a whole is "artificial," or controlled exclusively by subjective principles, whether logical or æsthetic.[1] The physical sciences have in the end to submit to experimental verification or the test of prediction. Only experience can establish their truth. "Empirical" laws and hypotheses are determined altogether by the "brute facts" of sensation. Exact theories, such as those of mechanics and mathematical physics, are not to be proved or disproved in the same decisive manner, but choice is made among them according to their *simplicity* and *convenience*. Theories upon this level are always subject to change, while empirical laws remain relatively constant. Theories are like languages or standards of measurement, alternative modes of representing the facts, which are all true so far as they *do* represent the facts; and supersede one another according as they prove better capable of representing these facts, and of assimilating new facts, without devious and unnecessary complications. So far as they cover the same facts, it will always be possible to translate these alternative theories into terms of one another, and thus exhibit their common nucleus of empirical truth. But Euclidean geometry, for example, offers a simpler account of human experience, and is a more convenient tool for creatures who are compelled to deal with an environment of rigid and solid bodies, than non-Euclidean geometry, even though the latter contains an equivalent of every expression of the former.

[1] Cf. his refutation of Le Roy, *La Valeur de la Science*, part III, and below, § 24.

What are these facts to which science is thus accountable in the last resort? Sensations are subjective, private, and variable. That which is common, communicable, and durable is the relationship among them. This order of connections is the only objective reality. Physical objects are no more than persistent relations among sensible qualities; and, similarly, scientific constructions, such as the ether, represent the fact that there is a natural *kinship* among all optical phenomena.[1]

We thus find in Poincaré a not wholly consistent combination of two views of the relations of knowledge to reality. On the one hand, science conforms itself to given facts, and rests on an experimental basis; while, on the other hand, it obeys an intuition of the inherent power of the mind and a taste for simplicity and harmony. It can be explained only as resultant of these two factors. There is a similar and wholly unreconciled duality in his ultimate philosophy of life. Science cannot affect morality, since the latter determines our ends and the former only our choice of means. But the only worthy ends are those æsthetic and rational ends whose supreme exemplification is found in science. Thought is only an episode in nature, and yet so far as nature is not thought—it is nothing.[2]

§ 12. Sociological Positivism. Durkheim

It has been remarked that naturalism tends by rejecting the divine to exalt the human. A desire to find

[1] *Op. cit.*, pp. 270, 271.   [2] *Op. cit.*, pp. 4, 275, 276.

some substitute for the ideals and absolutes of the opposite philosophy leads to a special emphasis on society, because this provides some human sanction of truths or of values beyond the individual. This tendency culminated in the nineteenth century in the sociological positivism or "sociologism" of France, and its most important representative was ÉMILE DURKHEIM,[1] who was born in Paris in 1858, inaugurated university instruction in sociology in Bordeaux in 1887, and was called in 1902 to the Sorbonne, where he was professor of the science of education from 1906 until his death in 1917. Durkheim's [2] teachings have led to the creation of a school which constitutes one of the major tendencies of contemporary French thought.[3] His influence was due in part to his commanding personality, in part to the bold and constructive character of his doctrines, and in part to their fertility for sociological research.

Of the genuinely philosophical character of these doc-

[1] This movement is continuously related to Comte. The forerunner of Durkheim was Alfred Espinas (1844–1922; *Les Sociétés animales*, 1876). While Espinas anticipated Durkheim in his emphasis on the organic unity of society, Gabriel Tarde (1843–1904; *Les Lois d'Imitation*, 1890) proposed to explain society in terms of "inter-psychology," or the influence of mind on mind through the force of imitation. The racial factor in sociology, together with the social application of Darwinian conceptions, was emphasized by Joseph Arthur Comte de Gobineau (1816–1882), and the psychology of the crowd by Gustave Le Bon (b. 1841; *La Psychologie des Foules*, 1895).

[2] His most important writings were: *De la Division du Travail social*, 1893; *Les Règles de la Méthode sociologique*, 1894; *Les Formes élémentaires de la Vie religieuse*, 1912 (English trans., *The Elementary Forms of the Religious Life*, 1915).

[3] Its most eminent representative on the philosophical, as distinguished from the strictly sociological, side is Lucien Lévy-Bruhl (b. 1857): *Morale et la Science des Mœurs*, 4th ed., 1910 (English trans., *Ethics and Moral Science*, 1905); *Fonctions mentales dans les Sociétés inférieures* (1910); *La Mentalité primitive*, 1922.

trines there can be no doubt. Society for Durkheim was not a mere incident of evolution, to be assimilated to more fundamental laws of nature, but a being *sui generis*, which is to be taken as the centre and point of departure for human knowledge. Truth owes its objective and authoritative quality to the fact that it is an expression of collective, as distinguished from individual, thought. The fundamental concepts of science, such as space and time, are "collective representations," or products of social experience arising as the necessary conditions of religious rites and other forms of concerted action. Even the fundamental principles of logic, such as those of contradiction and identity, reflect the peculiar needs of civilized society, as is proved by their absence in the "prelogical" and "mystical" mentality of primitive man.[1] That difference which rationalists have emphasized between the universality of the principles of knowledge and the particularity and relativity of sense is thus to be accounted for in terms of the difference between the common, impersonal mind, and the private, capricious mind of the individual. Nor is the content of the collective mind to be reduced to that of individual minds, either through their psychological interaction or through the accumulation of ancestral habits. Societies are irreducible entities, which have to be studied in their own terms and can be compared only with one another. It is true that societies embrace and are composed of individuals; but once constituted, they behave in a manner peculiar to themselves. They have a property, which like those of chemical sub-

[1] *Formes élémentaires de la Vie religieuse*, p. 18. Cf. Lévy-Bruhl, *op. cit.*

stances, is irreducible to the properties of their component elements.

This unique property of a social fact, by which it is distinguished from every other fact, is *constraint*, or *obligation*. In other words, society is primarily a moral or religious (and not, as is sometimes supposed, a biological or economic) entity. Hence the importance for Durkheim of ethics and comparative religion. Morality consists of certain established rules or customs, peculiar to a given historical group, and having a peculiar coercive power upon its members, who feel it to be at one and the same time both *of* them and *over* them. It is not a wholly external restraint, but rather the object of disinterested devotion. The moral good which the individual acknowledges is neither his own private good nor the private good of any other man, but something which he feels to be both immanent and transcendent, the very essence of himself and yet lying on a plane wholly different from that of any merely individual life. Morality is, therefore, not a calculation of individual interests, as the utilitarian would have it, nor an ideal formulation of what ought to be, but a social force and social fact that is capable, like other facts, of scientific description.[1] In other words, the group is a law to its members, and the standard of value is the genius of the group. Although this view evidently has conservative implications, it does not, Durkheim thought, cut off the possibility of criticism and reform. For there are aberrations and abnormalities which the group conscience will condemn; and there is a manifest destiny

[1] Cf. Lévy-Bruhl, *Morale et la Science des Mœurs*.

for each society, which its enlightened members will perceive, and which by the light of reason they will confirm and promote.[1]

The most profound manifestation of social life is religion. This does not consist of beliefs, traceable, as Spencer and others had proposed, to the individual's experience of nature or to his ghostly dreams; but of the force which men feel in the exaltation of the collective religious experience. The most primitive religious idea is the distinction between the *sacred* and the *profane*. Sacred objects, like the totem, are symbols of the group, and are invested with the power and awfulness which the group possesses for its members. Religion, like morality, rests on the postulate that "*society can be considered as a personality qualitatively different from the individual personalities which compose it.*" [2]

§ 13. The Influence of Recent Science

In any given epoch of human thought, philosophical naturalism will reflect those scientific generalizations which have altered the common beliefs of men, whether through redrafting the cosmic picture or through reconstituting the fundamental habits of the mind. Thus the naturalism of the nineteenth century reflected the great scientific doctrines of mechanism, atomism, evolution, and the conservation of energy; and the great scientific methods of experiment and description. The opening

---

[1] Durkheim's most important pronouncement on moral questions is his paper on "La Détermination du Fait moral," in *Bulletin de la Société française de Philosophie*, 1906.

[2] *Op. cit.*, p. 115.

decades of the twentieth century have witnessed another revolution in science of the sort that will inevitably beget a new type of naturalism. There is nothing new or philosophically significant in the continuing progress of scientific discovery, or in the increasing utility of its technological applications. Whatever moral is to be drawn from these aspects of science has long since been discounted and assimilated to the modern European philosophy of life. Nor is there anything radically new in the continuous refinement of the mathematical and physical instruments of research, unless it be a growing recognition of the extent to which the results of science depend on technic, and may therefore be regarded as in Poincaré's sense "conventional." The novelty of the new science lies not so much in the realm of method as in the realm of theory, affecting the constitution and order of the cosmos. It is unquestionably true that the general physiognomy of nature is already so altered as to be scarcely recognizable by one who is familiar only with its nineteenth-century portraits. What the new naturalism is to be, it would be folly to predict. The new theories have sprung up in different quarters more or less independently of one another, and yet are so radical and far-reaching that each will require to be corrected in the light of the rest before they can be said to form anything approaching a coherent system. This task of reconstruction, which must be left to science itself, is scarcely begun. The new theories demand, furthermore, so profound an alteration in every-day ideas and images, that it will require decades and perhaps centuries of re-education be-

NATURALISM AND POSITIVISM

fore common-sense can assimilate them and realize the cosmos which they delineate.[1]

Already the latest scientific revolution seems to have had two effects upon popular and philosophical thought: a new sense of cosmic immensity and complexity, and an obsolescence of Cartesian dualism.

The new cosmography has greatly increased the range of scientific knowledge both in space and in time. The physical universe is now measured in terms of "light-years" (the distance travelled by light in one year), a unit where magnitude is appreciated when it is realized that light reaches the earth from the sun in eight minutes. The planetary system to which the earth belongs is conceived as part of the Milky Way, which together with "suburban" star-clusters has a diameter of, perhaps, 200,000 light-years. Far beyond this region lie the so-called "spiral nebulæ" which make up the rest of the cosmos. The theory of the curvature of space, which is one of the possible corollaries of the theory of relativity, has suggested that the cosmos is finite, and that light traverses its circumference and returns to its origin in a definitely measurable time, such as a thousand million years. The margin of error in such calculations is proportional to their magnitude, but, however doubtful and inaccurate, they have already altered the extensive scale of the human imagination.

---

[1] The most fundamental of the new theories are those of relativity, the constitution of the atom, and cosmography. There is already an extensive literature on each of these topics, both popular and technical. The beginner will find the following books useful as introductions: B. Russell, *The A B C of Atoms*, 1924, and *The A B C of Relativity*, 1925; C. G. Abbott, *The Earth and Stars*, 1925; H. Shapley, *Starlight*, 1926.

There has been a similar tendency in the minimal direction. The atom, once conceived as a physical ultimate, has now become a system of electrons. Chemical elements are no longer irreducible. But in the case of the small as well as in the case of the great there is an increased sense of having reached a limit *at last*, in the unit of electricity. The quantum theory teaches that energy or "action" (energy multiplied by time) is also discrete, or composed of irreducible pulses. Both electrons and quanta are measurable, the electron, for example, being reckoned as having a diameter equal to one hundred-thousandth of its atomic orbit, which is one hundred-millionth of a centimetre.

Thus, at the same time that the totality of the cosmos has become greater, its elements have become smaller; and this change of scale is accompanied in both cases by an increase of definiteness. Instead of the idea of the immeasurably great or small, or of magnitudes exceeding comprehension, the new scientific theories suggest a cosmos which in bulk is measurably greater and in components measurably smaller than any cosmos hitherto conceived. The effect is both the sense of vastness, intricacy, and human dependence, and also the sense of an increased range and grasp on the part of the human mind.

A second general feature of the new naturalism which is already recognizable is the questioning of the Cartesian dualism.[1] Modern naturalism has hitherto emphasized the duality between the realm of inert and extended bodies, governed by physico-chemical (me-

[1] Cf. also § 30.

chanical) laws, and the realm of life and mind, governed by instinct, purpose, or thought; and has undertaken in some measure to reduce the second to the first. The present tendency is to view the duality itself as gratuitous and false, and the very variety of the motives at work testifies to the strength of the tendency.

Thus the theory of relativity has introduced a new conception of the relations of time and space, which suggests that physical things must be conceived not as essentially spatial and accidentally temporal, but as essentially *spatio-temporal*, as is the case with events, activities, and histories. Again, the idea that spatial, temporal, and mechanical properties, hitherto thought reducible to direct relations of position between matter and the absolute space and time which it occupies, are relative to the position and motion of the observer, introduces into the physical world itself that character of perspective or point of view which has been thought peculiar to perception. This change of view has reinforced the tendency already so marked in positivism, to identify nature with the actual or possible content of sensible experience. At the same time, neo-vitalism,[1] while representing a minority party in biology, has served to accentuate the difficulty of reducing the phenomena of life to physico-chemical terms, and has brought clearly to light the factor of organization. This emphasis, in turn, has seemed to point in one or the other of two directions. According to one view, the idea of organization serves as a connecting link between the corporeal and incorporeal worlds, or as a generic fea-

[1] § 22.

ture of nature in which the old Cartesian duality disappears. According to a second view, commonly known as "emergent evolution,"[1] the difference between organic and inorganic phenomena is only a special case of the sort of difference that occurs throughout nature on many levels. It is found lower in the scale in the difference between the physical and the chemical, and higher in the scale in the difference between the biological and the psychological. The result of the first view is that nature becomes homogeneous, and the result of the second view is that it becomes a graded series; but in either case the Cartesian duality loses its unique and central significance.

It is a further effect of contemporary science, in so far as it ceases to provide arguments for body *against* mind, or for mechanism *against* purpose, that naturalism should cease to be a partisan philosophy and should tend to merge with philosophies of other types. This effect is especially notable in the rapprochement between naturalism and realism.[2]

[1] The principal exponent of this view in naturalistic circles is C. LLOYD MORGAN (b. 1852; *Emergent Evolution*, 1923). Cf. also the writings of the English biologist, J. A. Thomson.

[2] As exemplified in the thought of B. Russell, A. N. Whitehead, and others (cf. § 29).

PART III

SPIRITUALISM AND IDEALISM

§ 14. Spiritualism in Germany. Fechner. Lotze. Hartmann

Although naturalism of either the materialistic or the positivistic variety was the dominant feature of German philosophy just after the middle of the nineteenth century, spiritualism and idealism had never been without their powerful advocates. Kant, whose *Critique of Pure Reason* had seemed to overthrow their claims, had, in his acknowledgment of the independent validity of the moral and æsthetic forms of consciousness, really placed new weapons in their armory. The great romanticists and idealists, Fichte, Hegel, Schopenhauer, and Schleiermacher, attended by a large following of lesser men, assured the continuity and prestige of the philosophy which championed the cause of the moral and religious tradition against the disparaging or destructive attacks made in the name of science. But while the pretensions of naturalism were thus disputed, the influence of science was felt even among those who refused to accept it as a philosophy. There was a general opinion that philosophy must make an adequate provision for the physical world, and that if it is possible to learn about nature from mind, it is no less possible to learn about mind from nature. This feeling led to a search for some common term by which both worlds might be interpreted.[1]

Nature, according to this view, does not, as in ideal-

---

[1] This tendency was exemplified by A. TRENDELENBURG (1802–1872), who found such a common term in *movement*. Cf. his *Logische Untersuchungen*, 1840.

ism, derive its relation to mind from the fact that it is an object of knowledge, but from the fact that it is inherently spiritual in substance, and is governed by purposes and ends rather than by merely mechanical laws. The spiritualistic philosophy is, in other words, objectivistic and speculative, after the manner of Aristotle and Leibniz, and in continuation of the later phases of Schelling. Spirituality is a fact discovered by metaphysics, rather than an assumption deduced by theory of knowledge. This method of attack, in which philosophy begins with nature, and construes nature objectively, rather than in terms of its relation to the knowing subject, signified the influence of the cult of science even on philosophers of the school opposed to naturalism. Just as materialism offered compromises with spiritualism, through its emphasis on force and life, so spiritualism made concessions to materialism by acknowledging the existence of an external and independent natural order.

GUSTAV THEODORE FECHNER, who was born in 1801 in Lauwitz, Germany, was a student of physics and of medicine, and in 1835 became professor of physics in Leipsic. His failing eyesight forced him eventually to abandon this professorship, and was one of the motives inducing him to turn in the direction of psychology and eventually of metaphysical speculation. As a scientist his most important achievement was the so-called "Weber-Fechner Law,"[1] according to which the intensity of sensation, instead of increasing in direct propor-

---

[1] Named "Weber's Law" by Fechner himself, in honor of his teacher, the physiologist, E. H. Weber. It can be most simply expressed by saying that the intensity of sensation increases as the logarithm of the stimulus.

tion to the strength of the stimulus, increases by diminishing increments; in other words, the stronger the existing stimulus the less will be the increase of sensation caused by an additional unit of stimulus.[1] This law marks the foundation of the branch of knowledge known as "psycho-physics"; and the exact, quantitative method used by him to establish it gives its author an important place in the history of experimental psychology.[2] In his *Atomenlehre* he agreed that, since physics conceives atoms only as *loci* of force or energy, there is no reason to assume that the ultimate constituents of the physical world are material or extended. Thus Fechner's scientific studies supported the view that there is definite correlation between the psychical and the physical, and that the physical may be interpreted as inwardly psychical. This doctrine of psycho-physical

[1] Cf. the *Elemente der Psychophysik* (1860). The more important of his other works are: *Zend-Avesta*, 1851; *Über die Seelenfrage*, 1861; *Die drei Motive des Glaubens*, 1863; *Über die physikalische und die philosophische Atomenlehre*, 1855; *Vorschule der Æsthetik*, 1876; *Die Tagesansicht gegenüber der Nachtansicht*, 1879; *Das Büchlein vom Leben nach dem Tode*, 1836 (English trans., *The Little Book of Life after Death*, 1912).

[2] Among the pioneers of this general movement, leading to the establishment of psychological laboratories in Europe and America, the following, in addition to Fechner, are especially worthy of mention: H. Helmholtz (§ 1) and Wilhelm Wundt (1832–1920), in Germany; W. James (§ 25) and G. Stanley Hall (1846–1924), in America. Wundt was an encyclopædic thinker who on his philosophical side may properly be classed with the present group, as maintaining a spiritualistic realism in which he aims to do justice to the scientific view of nature. As with Fechner, Lotze, and von Hartmann, so with Wundt, psychological knowledge, in the sense of the immediate revelation of consciousness, is superior to other sorts of knowledge, and justifies the belief that all reality is essentially psychical reality, namely, will. His chief philosophical writings were *Ethik*, 1886 (English trans., *Ethics*, 3 vols., 1897–1901); *System der Philosophie*, 1889, and *Einleitung in die Philosophie*, 1901. In America the influence of Wundt's philosophy was represented by G. T. Ladd (1842–1921), while the influence of his psychology is represented pre-eminently by E. B. Titchener.

idealism or "panpsychism," and the companion doctrine of the plurality and hierarchy of souls, were developed with great eloquence and speculative ingenuity in the most famous of his works, the *Zend-Avesta;* and their religious and moral implications absorbed his attention up to the time of his death in 1887. Although his temper of mind was strongly empirical, both doctrines led him far beyond the limits of exact observation, and involved the free use of the argument from analogy. He conceived reality in *terms* of experience, but he did not hesitate to transcend the field of *actual* experience. At the same time his ardent temperament led him to conclusions which he could justify only by their emotional appeal, and which he candidly acknowledged to be acts of faith.[1]

The difference between the physical and the psychical, according to Fechner, is a difference of point of view. That which *to itself* is psychical is *to others* physical. In other words, the physical is the phenomenal or extrinsic appearance of things. Behind the phenomenon lies not a dark unknowable, or an inert matter, but a psychical life like our own. All things are inwardly or intrinsically psychical. The physical and psychical are not, as in the "identity theory" of Spinoza, two aspects of a third and substantial principle, but the psychical is the substance and the physical is the aspect. This relation is in philosophical speculation extended by analogy to all of nature, and all bodily phenomena may be assumed to be or belong to the outward aspect of some soul.

[1] *Die Tagesansicht*, p. 78.

But Fechner was no more a Leibnizian monadist than he was a Spinozistic monist. Souls are possessed not by each distinguishable physical element or phenomenon, but only by such systems or organizations of phenomena as form organic wholes, like the bodies of plants and animals. The evidence of a spiritual reality behind phenomena is to be found in their orderly connection.[1] There are, in other words, bodies in the physical sense which have no souls of their own, but are only *constituents* of bodies in the biological and psycho-physical sense. Fechner believed, however, that not only plants and animals, but also the earth, the stars, and the total cosmos, are "bodies" of this type; and that one may, therefore, properly speak of an "earth-soul," and of a "soul of the world." God is this soul of the world, or the all-inclusive system of nature as it is to itself.

The relation of these souls to one another is a relation of inclusion. Just as the bodily man is a part of the physical system of the earth, so the soul of man is a part of the earth-soul, and the earth-soul in turn is a part of the soul of the world. As the soul of man embraces its diverse sensations and ideas within one synthetic unity, so the souls of all creatures are enveloped and unified within the soul of God. This may be otherwise expressed by saying that the soul of God is related to the soul of man as the ground swell to the waves which it carries. Because of its comparatively high threshold,[2] man's consciousness contains only fragments

---

[1] In their *"Zusammenhang"* and *"Gesetzmässigkeit."* Cf. *Über die Seelenfrage*, p. 268; *Zend-Avesta*, vol. I, p. 343.

[2] As proved by Weber's Law, which shows that there are intensities of physical stimulation which induce no psychical changes.

of the soul of God, the rest possessing to man only the aspect of externality, or body. God not only embraces the intermittent and isolated consciousnesses of all creatures, but gives organic unity and inward psychical nature to the dead past and to the inorganic stretches of nature. All of nature belongs to God's body, and is the outward manifestation of one psychical continuum, which is God's soul.[1]

RUDOLPH HERMANN LOTZE, the most distinguished and widely influential German philosopher during the latter half of the nineteenth century, was born in Bautzen in 1817. Like Fechner, his early training as well as his mature interests was divided between science and philosophy. At Leipsic he studied medicine and physics, and in philosophy came under the influence of Weisse. His numerous writings reflect the wide range of his studies. In his *Medical Psychology* (*Medizinische Psychologie*, 1852) he made important contributions, both physiological and speculative, to this new branch of science, his most notable theory being that of "local signs." This theory attributes to each sensory stimulation and to the motor response which it excites, a unique quality by which the datum of sense is assigned its proper place in the spatial system which the mind constructs. Lotze's most popular book was the *Microcosmus* (*Mikrokosmus*, 1856–1864), a work notable for its brilliancy of exposition and moral eloquence, in which the author dealt broadly with man—his natural constitution, his culture, and his destiny. His *History of*

[1] *Elemente der Psychophysik*, vol. II, p. 529.

He was essentially a speculative metaphysician, who wished to reveal the real world in all its manifold aspects. To this end he did not hesitate to employ and credit both sense-perception and reason, or to transcend both at the instigation of feeling and under the sanction of faith. The richness of his experience and the versatility of his genius led him to touch human life and culture at many points; and though it is easy to convict him of inconsistency, or even of dogmatism, his thought was more fruitful and stimulating to posterity than that of any other German thinker of his times.

All of our knowledge, said Lotze, reposes, in the last analysis, on a faith in reason. There is nothing by which reason can be corrected save itself. Even the sceptic, in the affirmation of his doubts, betrays some ultimate and indemonstrable conviction.[1] Ultimate convictions assume one of three forms. "All our analysis of the cosmic order ends in leading our thought back to a consciousness of necessarily valid *truths*, our perception to the intuition of immediately given *facts* of reality, our conscience to the recognition of an absolute standard of all *determinations of worth*."[2] These convictions are independent of one another. Necessary truths do not yield facts, nor facts necessity; and neither necessity nor fact follows from the apprehension of value. The synthesis of these three forms of knowledge, in the conception of a *universe which embraces the acts under necessary laws and realizes the norms of value*, is again an act of faith. Philosophy cannot be expected to do more

[1] *Logik* of 1874, § 305.
[2] *Microcosmus*, English trans., book IX, § 2.

SPIRITUALISM AND IDEALISM

Æsthetics (*Geschichte der Æsthetik in Deutschland,* 1868) was also widely read, and has exercised a notable influence in this field, especially through his anticipation of the theory of "empathy" (*Einfühling*), according to which the enjoyment of æsthetic forms, such as symmetry, is occasioned by the perception of corresponding movements and tensions in the organism.[1] The most mature formulation of his system is to be found in the *Logic* (*Logik*, 1874), and in the *Metaphysics* (*Metaphysik*, 1879), written while the author was a professor at Göttingen. A third volume was to have dealt with æsthetics, ethics, and philosophy of religion, but its completion was prevented by the author's death in 1881, a year after he had been called to the University of Berlin.[2]

Although Lotze was trained in science and sought a reconciliation of science and philosophy, and although he was a most thorough and painstaking thinker, he was neither a rigorous scientist nor a critical philosopher. He had nothing of that cautious temper which is content with meagre results, provided they are methodically correct. He was not greatly interested in theory of knowledge, which he compared to "the tuning of instruments before a concert."[3] Though he created a comprehensive system he was more interested in its comprehensiveness than in its systematic coherence.

[1] *Geschichte der Æsthetik,* pp. 76–79. Cf. *Medizinische Psychologie,* p. 293.
[2] His other important philosophical works were: *Metaphysik*, 1841, and *Logik*, 1843 (not to be confused with the works of 1874 and 1879); *Kleine Schriften*, composed of shorter articles and reviews, published posthumously. Works mentioned in the text have been translated into English as follows: *Microcosmus*, 1884; *Logic*, 1884; *Metaphysics*, 1884.
[3] *Metaphysics,* Introduction, § ix.

than to elaborate this conception, and to remove objections that stand in the way of its acceptance.

There are necessary truths which represent the nature of reason itself, and which it is the business of logic to formulate. These truths express themselves in the form of propositions, and, together with their component concepts, and the trains of reasoning into which they enter, they possess for Lotze a peculiar status of "validity" (*Geltung*), which is to be sharply distinguished from that of existence. The major fault of ancient philosophy was the confusion of logic and metaphysics, or the supposition that concepts are things and that the relations among concepts in thought are the same as the relations among things in reality. It is this very independence on existence that gives thought its freedom and constructive capacity; but this independence is reciprocal, and existence, not being subject to thought, can be known only by experience. It is experience which determines what proposition, being logically consistent or in agreement with the necessary truths of reason, shall also be true *of*, or valid *for*, reality. It has been assumed as a part of the fundamental trust in the possibility of knowledge, that reality does so lend itself to being known in terms of logic; but *which* among the logical possibilities is applicable to reality, is discoverable only through the action of reality upon our minds in sensation.

Lotze does not deduce the nature of reality either from logical premises (after the manner of rationalism) or from the *a priori* conditions of knowledge (after the manner of idealism). He thinks empirically and realistically of an independently given world to which the scientist and the metaphysician (unlike the logician) must accommodate themselves. But he believes that it is a part of the task of philosophy to show how it happens that reality agrees with the forms of logic, and how it happens that it can be known empirically. He finds an answer to both questions in the nature of reality as represented by physical nature. As an orderly system of relations, reality can be known by logical thought, the propositions that are *true* of it being projections, variations, or approximations of the laws that *hold* of it. As a field of interacting substances, of which the mind is itself one, reality can be known empirically, sense-perception being a special case of reciprocity. Perceptions are subjective, as are space and time in their perceptual form, but they are appropriate *reactions* which fit the actions which evoke them, as the sword fits the scabbard, or as the meshes of the net fit the objects which are caught in it.[1]

Lotze's metaphysics starts with the mechanical conception of nature, as a system of interacting corporeal units. These units, or atoms, as ultimate and indivisible, have to be considered as active rather than as extended. Nor is their plurality to be regarded as a final view of their relations. For action and reaction are inconceivable if the interacting elements are independent. That one element should change in consequence of changes in another element implies that they are in reality only phases of one underlying substance, so unitary in nature that its several states are all reciprocal

[1] *Microcosmus*, English trans., 2d ed., vol. II, p. 349.

and compensatory. Since all of the elements of reality react to one another in a way that is determined, we must conclude that the nature of each is implicated in the nature of the rest, or that all are parts of one substance or vitally connected whole. Thus Lotze's ultimate view of nature was *monistic* rather than *monadistic*.

Having concluded that reality is a single substance within which all changes are reciprocally determined, Lotze had now to establish its spiritual constitution. To be real in the physical sense is to stand in dynamic relations, that is, to maintain identity, while inducing or suffering change. But we cannot grasp the meaning of these characters save in terms of actual feeling, and in terms of the unity of consciousness. To say of anything that *it* acts or suffers, implies something more than a change of state antecedent or subsequent to changes of state in other things. It implies that it *itself* recognizes such changes as its own—as modes of its self-affirmation or of self-preservation. Only spiritual subjects exercise this function, and can be regarded as ultimately real.[1] Two such realities we are forced to recognize, namely, our finite selves and God, or the universal being which is the ground of nature. Whether there be over and above these realities a third order of natural substances cannot, Lotze thinks, be absolutely determined. For it is possible to suppose that the objects of nature are but the modes of God's activity upon our minds. But this reduction of nature to states induced in us by God cannot be argued, as idealists have con-

---

[1] *Microcosmus*, bk. IX, ch. III; *Metaphysics* (1879), bk. I, ch. VII.

tended, from the general fact of the relativity of knowledge. Whether there were or were not a real nature external to our minds we should, in any case, have to know it in terms of our own states. The realistic position is conceded in principle even by Fichte, in his admission of other spiritual beings, who, despite their externality to ourselves, are nevertheless known by us. Hence the reality of nature cannot be dismissed on any *a priori* grounds; and Lotze accepted it, with some hesitation, as affording the best explanation of sense-perception and of the facts of science. Metaphysics compels us to provide further for a universal spiritual substratum, or God, as the ground of nature.[1]

Lotze was primarily concerned to show that if nature is real, it must be thought of as consisting of spiritual beings below the level of man, and, like man, grounded in the universal substance of God. "Either only minds exist, and the whole world of things is a phenomenon in minds, or things which appear to us as permanent yet selfless points of departure, intersection, and termination of action, are beings which share with minds in various degrees the general characteristic of mentality, namely self-existence." Adopting the latter alternative, Lotze thought of nature as composed of beings which, while dependent on God in the sense of being modes of his activity, nevertheless exist themselves, as having both feeling and will, and in some measure that capacity for self-identification more fully manifested in the self-conscious ego.[2]

[1] *Metaphysics* (1879), §§ 94–97.
[2] *Microcosmus*, bk. IX, ch. III (English trans., 1887), vol. II, p. 657.

SPIRITUALISM AND IDEALISM

Lotze's philosophy of religion rests in part upon his spiritualistic metaphysics, which reveals God as the ultimate substance of things, and as possessing in a superlative degree that character of self-conscious personality which is the essential qualification for reality. But religion is primarily an expression of feeling rather than of intellect. It reflects, on the one hand, the feeling of dependence, and, on the other hand, the acknowledgment of beauty and goodness. It cannot, therefore, be judged in the last analysis by canons of theoretical truth. It embodies judgments of value (the "indemonstrable but irreversible declarations" of "conscience and feeling"), which are irreducible to judgments of fact or of logical necessity.[1] It expresses, furthermore, a faith in the ultimate synthesis of fact, necessity, and value. According to the view with which Lotze concluded his *Microcosmus*, and which he offers as a "confession of his philosophic faith," God is a single power, "appearing to us under a threefold image"—"namely, first some definite and desired Good, then on account of the definiteness of this, a formed and developing Reality, and finally in this activity an unvarying reign of Law."[2]

Thus Lotze represented a regard for scientific fact, a recognition of the universal necessities of thought, and,

---

[1] *Op. cit.*, p. 719. Through his insistence on the irreducibility of judgments of value to judgments of theoretic truth, Lotze is affiliated with that later form of idealism which would *reduce* the latter to the former (§ 79). Indeed, Lotze himself concluded his *Metaphysics* with the dictum that "the true beginning of Metaphysics lies in Ethics." Through his identification of religion with judgments of value, and his interpretation of dogmas in terms of their expression of religious experience, Lotze is related to the important movement in philosophy of religion of which the most distinguished leader was A. Ritschl (1822–1889).

[2] *Op. cit.*, p. 716.

beyond these, a speculative zeal for a metaphysical view which should satisfy not only the strictly intellectual demands, but the aspirations of man's moral, æsthetic, and religious nature.

The characteristics which are common to Fechner and Lotze appear again in EDUARD VON HARTMANN,[1] the most original among the disciples of Schopenhauer. Again we find a receptivity to science, combined with a willingness to supplement or reinterpret it by free speculation, and by the argument from analogy; again we find a general tendency to metaphysical realism, and the more specific tendency to overcome the dualism of the physical and mental worlds by construing nature as of the same substance with spirit.

Hartmann's most famous work, the *Philosophy of the Unconscious*, which had a wide vogue in the '70's, is an attempt to construct a new monism that shall escape the opposite errors of Hegel and Schopenhauer. The former, identifying the real with the rational, was unable to offer any satisfactory account of the irrational

---

[1] Born in 1842 in Berlin, died in 1906. Originally trained as an officer in the Prussian army, he retired for reasons of health, and became a private scholar, living in the neighborhood of Berlin. His most important work was the *Philosophie des Unbewussten*, 1869 (English trans., 1886). Among his other works are: *Kritische Grundlegung des transcendentalen Realismus*, 1875; *Phänomenologie des sittlichen Bewusstseins*, 1879; *Das religiöse Bewusstsein der Menschheit*, 1881. Among the German thinkers related to Hartmann through common descent from Schopenhauer, the following are deserving of mention: J. Frauenstädt (1813–1878; *Briefe über die Schopenhauersche Philosophie*, 1854; *Neue Briefe*, etc., 1876); Paul Deussen (1845–1919; *Elemente der Metaphysik*, 1877, English trans., 1894); Richard Wagner, the great composer (1813–1883; collected writings, 9 vols., 2d ed., 1887–1888); and Friedrich Nietzsche (§ 22).

and changing aspect of the world; while the latter, identifying the real with blind will, was equally unable to account for order and purpose. The reconciliation is to be found in the conception of a spiritual reality that partakes both of reason and of will. This principle is called "the Unconscious," because it underlies that very process of natural development in which consciousness itself appears. Hartmann accepted materialism, in other words, so far as this teaches that consciousness is conditioned by the brain, and argued that consciousness cannot be the cause of its own conditions. But the principle which produces the brain and the whole system of physical nature must nevertheless be regarded as spiritual because it exhibits intelligence. It resembles consciousness in that it acts *as if* it deliberately adopted ends and selected the means necessary to realize them. Spirit, being thus divorced from consciousness, may be identified with the "force" of physics. It explains the biological phenomena of growth and of intelligent, though unwitting, adaptation. Without invoking the Unconscious it is impossible to explain even the phenomena of consciousness; it is needed to account for instinct, for the bodily movements that do the bidding of volition, for the processes of sensation and association which underlie thought, for the spontaneity of human motives, for the co-operation of individuals in society, and for the fitting of man into the greater cosmic purposes which he serves more wisely than he knows.

As regards the issue between optimism and pessimism, Hartmann also attempted to mediate between Hegel and Schopenhauer. With the latter he held that existence is essentially evil, proceeding from the blindness of spirit, and not from its intelligence. The alliance of reason with will makes the existent world the best of all possible existents, but cannot negate the fact that to exist at all is evil, being invariably productive of more pain than pleasure. A purely rational principle would not have created at all. Since the world does exist, the best that reason can do to mitigate the fact is to produce consciousness, and develop it to the point at which the evil may be undone by the cessation of will.

Thus Hartmann's pessimism, close as it is to that of Schopenhauer, does nevertheless give a certain meaning to the course of natural and historical development, and so allies itself both with the doctrine of natural evolution and with the Hegelian philosophy of history. Development is retained in the form of a sort of progressive disillusionment which reveals, first, the vanity of the goods of this world; second, the vanity of hope of a future life; and, third, that crowning vanity of the modern world which believes that happiness can be attained in the distant future by the agencies of civilized society. It is the duty of the individual not to withdraw from this enterprise, and contrive a private salvation of his own, but to identify himself with it, and so to share the suffering by which the Unconscious is to be redeemed. It is God himself who has committed the initial "folly" of willing to exist, through an inexplicable lapse of reason, thus liberating in the world the evil principle of will. True morality and religion consist in the recognition of the evil of existence, together with a sympathy with God, and a willingness to share in the suffering by which God and the world with him shall at last be redeemed.

§ 15. **Spiritualism in France. Maine de Biran. Cousin. Ravaisson. Boutroux**

In turning from Germany to France we must recall to mind the state of philosophy in the latter country at the close of the eighteenth century. The characteristic features of the thought of this century had been derived from England, but had reached their most advanced development in France in the period of the Revolution. A reliance on the human understanding, together with a suspicion of mysticism, traditionalism, and authority; a tendency to construe the understanding in terms of sense-perception and observation, rather than in terms of *a priori* reason; a preoccupation with the psychology of knowledge, rather than with metaphysics, and an effort to trace ideas to experience through reducing them to sensations; an emphasis on the human individual, as opposed to all types of universal, whether abstract, metaphysical, or institutional; a confident belief in the possibility, through the spread of enlightenment, of reforming society and reconstituting the state: such was the prevailing creed. This creed was carried over from the eighteenth to the nineteenth century, or from the Revolutionary to the Napoleonic era, by the so-called "idealogues," represented by Cabanis and Destutt de Tracy, and so called because of their continuing Hume's and Condillac's studies of the sensory origin of ideas.[1]

[1] § 3.

The reaction against the creed of the eighteenth century took many forms, which may be grouped broadly under two major ideas. The first of these is the idea of *organic unity*—the idea (as opposed to individualism and revolution) that the human individual *belongs* to something greater than himself, such as the process of history, or the corporate institutions of Church and State, or the all-embracing cosmic Whole. The second idea is that of *spontaneity*, according to which man, instead of being merely the passive recipient of impressions from without, derives truth and authority from within, and finds the key to the interpretation of the world in the revelation of himself. It is evident that these two ideas, despite their common opposition to the creed of the eighteenth century, are in conflict with one another, in so far as the first inclines to a sense of dependence and the latter to a cult of freedom and self-exaltation. These two ideas and the conflict between them constituted a central *motif* of German philosophy in the first half of the nineteenth century.

To understand the course of French thought during the same epoch it is necessary to analyze further the second of these ideas, or that of spontaneity. In its broader cultural application this idea constitutes what is called "romanticism." But there is a narrower meaning of romanticism which is intelligible only in terms of a further distinction. The spontaneity of the mind may, on the one hand, have reference to its *cognitive* operations, and signify the fact that the mind supplies the forms or categories of knowledge from its own constitution. In this sense the Kant of the first *Critique* and all his idealistic followers were romanticists. But the spontaneity of the mind may, on the other hand, signify the priority of will and feeling to the necessities imposed by the intellect.[1] Romanticism in this narrower sense is the source, not of idealism, but rather of spiritualism. Nature is conceived not as the construction of the knowing mind, but as the outward manifestation of that essential reality which is directly revealed in activity and emotional aspiration.

Romanticism in this second and narrower sense was indigenous to French thought. It had received a powerful impulse from Rousseau, who, although an exponent of the mind of the eighteenth century, was also, in his protest against the extravagant claims of sensationalism and in his insistence that true morality and religion must spring from the "heart" rather than from the intellect, a major prophet of the age to come. French romanticism in the nineteenth century was thus originally a romanticism of the voluntaristic and sentimental type, bred by an internal reaction against the intellectualism of the eighteenth century. This indigenous impulse was thereafter confirmed by the intermittent influence of German romanticism of the same type, chiefly as represented by Schelling. At the same time, through the study of Kant, this current of thought was gradually blended with a romanticism of the intellectualistic and idealistic type. It remains, however,

---

[1] In this sense, it is the Kant of the second and third *Critiques* who is the romanticist. There is a still narrower sense of "romanticism" (represented by Schelling and the Schlegels as opposed to Fichte), in which it signifies the priority of *feeling* to the moral will or to the constraint of duty.

broadly characteristic of French philosophy in the nineteenth century that the tendency opposed to naturalism should have assumed the form of *spiritualism*.

The patron saint of French spiritualism in the nineteenth century was MAINE DE BIRAN, who, although he lived at the opening of the century, did not assume a place of high importance until fifty years later. He was born at Bergerac in 1766, and died in 1824, his life thus embracing both the Revolutionary and the Napoleonic eras. But he maintained a certain detachment from all the revolutionary changes of his time. He compared himself to a miner whose real life was spent in the subterranean depths of his own inner consciousness. His vocation was that of self-examination, in which he displayed that extraordinary delicacy of observation, and power to detect the nuance of a passing mood, which marked Rousseau, and is characteristic generally of modern French literature and psychology. He held no academic post, constructed no system of philosophy, published little, and owed his influence to his friendships, and to his rediscovery by a more sympathetic posterity.[1]

Maine de Biran's point of departure was the doctrine of the "idealogues,"[2] Cabanis and Destutt de Tracy, with whom he was intimately associated in the circle of Madame Helvetius at Auteuil in 1797. These thinkers had begun already to modify the traditional sensational-

---

[1] His only important publication during his life was *The Influence of Habit* (*L'Influence de l'Habitude*, 1802). His posthumous works are: *Nouvelles Considérations sur les Rapports du Physique et du Moral*, 1834; *Œuvres philosophiques*, 1841; *Œuvres inédites*, 1859; *Science et Psychologie*, 1887; *Œuvres*, 1920–1922.

[2] § 3.

ism of their school. Cabanis accepted instinct and unconscious dispositions as predetermining the mind's reception of impressions from without, while de Tracy insisted on the felt activity of will, as the source of the idea of an external world. Maine de Biran developed both of these ideas. Impressed with the power of temperament and uncontrollable moods to alter the whole current of the mental life, he conceived of a level of "pure affection," underlying conscious personality and intimately dependent on organic conditions. Self-consciousness emerges from these physiological depths, which can never be penetrated by clear introspection, but manifest themselves in somnambulism, or in the transition from the sleeping to the waking state, or in the twilight zone which surrounds the focus of attention. With the passivity of this subconscious mind is contrasted the essential *activity* of consciousness itself. We know ourselves only as active: "The same reflexive act by which the subject knows himself and calls himself 'I,' reveals him to himself as an acting force." The effects of my will I localize and distinguish from myself, but I could not thus localize my will itself without distinguishing it from myself and so destroying it.[1]

This free and self-identifying activity is the first principle not only of all psychology, but of all philosophy as well. It distinguishes waking consciousness from sleep, and the mental life of man from that of animals. As the basic certainty of knowledge Maine de Biran proposed to substitute for Descartes's famous *cogito ergo sum*, the proof: "*I feel or perceive myself free cause,*

[1] *Œuvres philosophiques*, 1841, vol. IV, pp. 244–245.

therefore I am really cause." ("*Je me sens ou m'aperçois cause libre, donc je suis réelement cause.*"[1]) This same self-activity furnishes the bridge to the external world, since the subject as acting force is known as exerting itself against resistance.[2] It is also the source of the categories, such as force, cause, unity, and identity, by which we understand the world. It preserves the individual existences from being merged in a unity of substance, and establishes a polar relation between the personality of man the created and God the creative force.[3]

As in his earlier thought he opposed the active personal mind to the passive animal mind, so in his later thought Maine de Biran provided for a still higher level of mind, or "mystical life of enthusiasm"—a longing for ideal perfection, in which the soul is reunited with God.[4] Even in this religious phase of his thought he sought to obtain through spiritual exercises, prayer, and meditation, the confirming evidence of an inner experience.

Maine de Biran recognized the outstanding difficulty of his philosophy. In immediate self-consciousness I know beyond doubt my own existence as active force, and the correlative resistance of something external to my self. But this revelation does not yield an enduring order of existence beyond my momentary and relative experiences. To complete his philosophy, Maine de Biran thus felt the necessity of invoking what he called

---

[1] *Œuvres philosophiques*, p. 249.
[2] *Œuvres inédites*, vol. I, pp. 47–48.
[3] *Œuvres philosophiques*, vol. III, p. 20.
[4] *Œuvres inédites*, vol. III, pp. 541, 571.

"belief," a faculty which apprehends the absolute, and provides a framework of reality into which the deliverances of the individual consciousness can be fitted.[1] This need of finding an escape for metaphysical purposes from the limitations of the psychological method becomes the dominant motive in the philosophy of Cousin.

Unlike Maine de Biran, VICTOR COUSIN exercised a profound influence upon his times, but has been more lightly esteemed by posterity. His influence was due as much to the circumstances of his career, and his relation to his times, as to the quality of his genius. Born in 1792, he became professor at the Sorbonne in 1815, and from 1830 to 1851, as director of the École Normale Supérieure and minister of state, he became a sort of educational dictator, being thus enabled to give to his teachings an official sanction and prestige of orthodoxy. To the influence of position was added an eloquence and enthusiasm which made the delivery of his famous lectures on *The True, the Beautiful, and the Good* in 1818 a memorable event in the lives of his contemporaries.[2] His learning and keen interest in the history of philosophy, and his acquaintance with the thought of Germany, gained through his studies and travels in that

[1] Cf. *Science et Psychologie*, pp. 163–186.
[2] This work (*Du Vrai, du Beau, et du Bien*) was first published in 1837, and later reissued in a succession of revised editions. It was translated into English in 1853. His *Œuvres complètes* were published in 22 volumes, 1846–1847. Other works translated into English: *Elements of Psychology*, 1856; *History of Modern Philosophy*, 1852; *Philosophy of the Beautiful*, 1849. Cousin's thought exerted a powerful influence in England and America, where it combined with German influences (especially that of Schelling) to provoke the romanticist tendency. He died in 1867, after his influence had already begun to wane.

country, greatly broadened the outlook of French philosophy. Above all, he satisfied the need, so keenly felt in his epoch after years of disillusionment and narrow empiricism, for an edifying and inspiring creed, and for a philosophy on the grand scale.

The school of Cousin is commonly known as "eclecticism," signifying an acceptance of the essential truths contained in all the great systems of the past, and their union in one all-embracing system. In opposition to the destructive temper of scepticism and the cautious temper of empiricism, the term implies a disposition to credit as at least partially true all of the ideas which have obtained a strong hold upon human belief. In opposition to original speculation, it implies that the office of philosophy is architectonic rather than creative.

But Cousin saw, nevertheless, that the true historic doctrines cannot be distinguished from the false without some independent criterion, and that they cannot be combined without being re-thought. He preferred, therefore, to regard himself as the exponent of "spiritualism," the philosophy which is "the natural ally of all good causes."[1] This philosophy he sought to establish by the study of the mind, or by psychology, which he regarded as the "grand method of modern philosophy,"[2] inaugurated by Descartes. The empiricists, Locke and Condillac, who have followed the psychological method, are to be preferred to those who, like Spinoza, have departed from it; but while they are to be praised for their psychology they are to be condemned

---

[1] *Du Vrai, du Beau, et du Bien*, edition of 1881, p. iv.
[2] *Ibid.*, p. 3.

SPIRITUALISM AND IDEALISM

for their empiricism. They have construed the mind too narrowly in terms of sensibility and have neglected the reason. Among those who have by a deepening of the psychological method brought to light the universal and necessary principles on which science and metaphysics, religion and common-sense, alike repose, Reid was "the most irreproachable," and Kant "the most systematic."[1] Cousin had made the acquaintance of the Scottish philosopher Reid, through his teacher and acknowledged master Roger Collard,[2] and with the former's cast of mind, as well as with his doctrines, he always felt a peculiar affinity.

To Kant, Cousin devoted considerable attention. He credited him with having shown by the psychological method that space, time, causality, substance, and the other categories are necessary principles of reason underived from sense. He condemned him, however, for having attached these principles to the human mind and limited their application to the sphere of sensation. The outcome of Kant's view is a scepticism even more destructive than that scepticism of Hume which he had undertaken to overthrow. The principles of reason are not mere subjective necessities. They appear to be so only when in *reflection* the mind finds itself incapable of rejecting them. Reflection is a secondary process of mind, which implies a direct and positive apprehension of principles, a "spontaneous intuition," "a sphere of light and of peace where reason perceives the truth . . . because God has made reason to perceive it as he has made the eye to see."[3] This spontaneous intuition is

[1] *Du Vrai, du Beau, et du Bien*, p. 13. [2] § 3. [3] *Ibid.*, pp. 40, 41, 61.

the true logic of nature, which is revealed, as Reid had rightly maintained, to common-sense, and which neither needs nor is capable of any proof. These same principles lead us to God,[1] for they cannot be thought either to exist by themselves or to reside in particular existences, or in the human mind. They are the thoughts of God, reflected in the laws of nature, and serving as a link between man and God.[2]

Although Cousin represented the romantic reaction against the eighteenth century, and regarded himself as the champion of the spiritualistic revival, he was promptly repudiated by the more advanced exponents of these very tendencies. His chief critic was FÉLIX RAVAISSON-MOLLIEN, whose *Report on Philosophy in France in the Nineteenth Century* (1867) contained a vigorous attack upon both eclecticism and positivism, and a new spiritualistic confession of faith. Ravaisson was born in 1813, and in his early youth came under the influence both of Cousin and of Schelling, whose lectures he attended at Munich.[3] He found his chief philosophical inspiration, however, in Aristotle, Leibniz, and, above all, in Maine de Biran, for whose canonization he was chiefly responsible. He was a man of profound erudition and wide experience, not only steeped in the history of philosophical and religious thought, but, as Curator of the Department of Antiquities in the

[1] As do conscience and the sense of beauty, by other routes.
[2] *Du Vrai, du Beau, et du Bien*, pp. 67–102.
[3] He here formed the acquaintance of CHARLES SECRÉTAN (1815–1895; *Philosophie de la Liberté*, 1848–1849), whose development was in many respects parallel to his own, and who became the most distinguished Swiss philosopher of the second half of the century.

Louvre from 1874 to his death in 1900, both a learned archæologist and an appreciative connoisseur in the field of the fine arts. His strictly philosophical writings were few, and like his German contemporaries of the romantic era he sought in philosophy not a technical solution of its own traditional problems, but rather a unified interpretation of all culture.[1]

To Ravaisson, Cousin's philosophy was only a "half-spiritualism" (*demi-spiritualisme*).[2] Cousin had, it is true, taken a step beyond empiricism by introducing the principles of reason, and by paying homage to the supremacy of spirit. But he had still proceeded, after the manner of the eighteenth century, to observe and analyze *ideas*. To sensations he had added abstract conceptions, but these bore no intelligible relation either to the soul, or to nature, or to God. Ideas conceived as passive states of the mind, whether of sensation or of reason, remained but external and disconnected appearances of some underlying reality whose nature remained unknown, and whose existence had to be dogmatically affirmed. What was needed was a metaphysical *insight* that should, on the one hand, reveal the essential nature of reality, and, on the other hand, serve as an explanatory key to the universe. This Ravaisson found neither in the inductive, observational method of the British and French schools of the eighteenth cen-

---

[1] Besides the above-mentioned *Report* (*Rapport sur la Philosophie en France*, 1867) his chief philosophical writings were: *De l'Habitude*, 1838 (*Revue de Métaphysique et de Morale*, 1894); *Essai sur la Métaphysique d'Aristote*, vol. I, 1837, vol. II, 1846; "Métaphysique et Morale," in *Revue des deux Mondes*, 1893.

[2] *Rapport sur la Philosophie en France*, p. 19.

tury, nor in the dialectic and intellectual intuition of the German schools of the nineteenth century, but in Maine de Biran. This writer, however, had not realized the full significance of his own discovery. He had pointed to the mind's immediate awareness of itself as will, but, by unduly stressing the experience of effort, he had failed to see that the essence of will is desire, and that desire is essentially aspiration or love—a striving toward perfection.

Spirit so construed furnishes the desired key by which the diverse aspects of reality and experience can be united. Spiritual activity is not an attribute of substance, it *is* substance: to be is to act.[1] To will and to think are the same thing, since thought is an *operation*, which aims to complete and unify experience: to be is to think.[2] When thought is thus construed as creative synthesis, there is no longer any division between knowledge and art.[3] Spirit, so conceived, is seen to be the essence of nature. The organic sciences have always found it necessary to employ the conception of finality, or to construe the parts in terms of the whole.[4] But even the inorganic sciences must in the end resort to the same spiritual categories. Inanimate nature differs from life and consciousness only in the *degree* of its spirituality. All movement is at bottom a *tendency*; inertia is a tendency to maintain or conserve motion.[5] This tendency for any activity to persist gives rise to habit; and the aspect of automatism presented by in-

---

[1] *Rapport*, p. 241.   [2] *Ibid.*, p. 259.   [3] *Ibid.*, p. 236.
[4] Referring to the ideas of Claude Bernard (§ 3).
[5] *Rapport*, pp. 249, 250, 254.

SPIRITUALISM AND IDEALISM

organic nature is to be construed, after the analogy of habit, as a degraded or fossilized will.[1] Only active and self-identical spirits can form habits, and nature can be understood only as a by-product of God. Physical nature is "a refraction or dispersion" of the divine spirit.[2] Unwilling to recognize any alien principle, and finding a purely negative principle unacceptable, Ravaisson conceives the inferior order of nature to be the voluntary product of God, who has deprived existence of perfection in order that it may seek and recover it.[3]

Spirit is both determined and free; determined in that the end is not possible without the means, which are its necessary conditions; free in that the end is desired and chosen, and is unpredictable from the means. It is only after the fact and regressively that the relation of antecedents to consequents can be seen to be necessary. In its forward direction change is governed by "a tendency to perfection, to good, and to beauty," which is the very essence of freedom, because it expresses the natural bias and true will of every creature.[4]

Ravaisson having designed and constructed the new spiritualism, ÉMILE BOUTROUX undertook to defend it against the rising tide of naturalism. Born in 1845, at Montrouge, he entered upon his career in that decade of the 60's when (despite the reign of eclecticism in official and academic circles) materialism and positivism were gaining many adherents in France as well as abroad. Science spoke with an authority that could

---

[1] Cf. the author's work, *De l'Habitude.*
[2] *Ibid.*, p. 255.   [3] *Ibid.*, pp. 262–263.   [4] *Ibid.*, pp. 250–254.

not be ignored; it was necessary to take cognizance of it and meet it on its own grounds. This Boutroux undertook to do in the most important of his books, *On the Contingency of the Laws of Nature*, published in 1874.[1] Like Ravaisson, he was conversant with contemporary thought in Germany, spending the years 1868–1870 as a student at Heidelberg. He exerted a direct personal influence upon his younger contemporaries through his teaching at the École Normale Supérieure and Sorbonne, and through his directorship (from 1902 until his death in 1922) of the Fondation Thiers.

There are, according to Boutroux, three types of necessity and determination that seem to exclude the reality of spirit, with its prerogative of freedom: logico-mathematical or deductive necessity, of the Cartesian type; categorical necessity, of the Kantian type; and empirical inductive uniformities, of the Humian type.[2] In each case, however, something is left *unnecessitated*, or "contingent." Deductive necessity leaves existence itself contingent, since it deals only with abstract possibilities, which may or may not be realized, and which if they *are* realized are never realized exactly.[3] Furthermore, even mathematics starts from unproved postulates, and as physics is not deducible from mathematics, so each successive science in the scale of complexity

---

[1] Translated into English in 1916, the French title being *De la Contingence des Lois de la Nature*. His other important works (all of which have been translated into English) were *De l'Idée de Loi naturelle dans la Science et la Philosophie contemporaines*, 1895; *Questions de Morale et d'Éducation*, 1895; *La Science et la Religion dans la Philosophie contemporaine*, 1908; and various studies in the history of philosophy.

[2] *De la Contingence*, etc., ch. I.   [3] *Ibid.*, ch. II.

presents novelties which are underivable from the last.[1] In the second place, Kant is correct in denying that nature imposes her laws upon our minds, but mistaken in supposing that our minds impose a set of predetermined categories upon nature. The categories themselves are an adaptation both of nature to mind and of mind to nature, an "accord" or "compromise" between the two.[2] There remains the empirical sequence of events, the routine of nature, in which an object is determined by the sum of its actual conditions. But here there is no necessity at all. The facts being given, we can grasp their relations and predict their recurrence; but we do not see why they must be so, nor could we have predicted their original occurrence. Our knowledge is of existences, but it is experimental and *a posteriori*. All of these elements of contingency increase as we rise in the hierarchy of the sciences from the more abstract level of mathematics to the more concrete levels of life and mind.

The element of contingency in science opens the way for metaphysics and invites its aid. From this point Boutroux restates and amplifies the thought of Ravaisson. That which from the standpoint of science is negative, a mere failure to complete its programme, is from the standpoint of metaphysics a positive and explanatory principle. Science admits contingency as a limiting factor, metaphysics construes it in terms of the free, creative activity of spirit. Spirit is that which is at once most concrete and most free. The failure of logic and

---

[1] *De la Contingence*, etc., ch. III–VII.
[2] *L'Idée de Loi naturelle*, pp. 137–139.

the plasticity of the categories may now be seen as due to their failure to express the whole of spirit, which is not mere intellect, but also feeling and will; having æsthetic and moral, as well as scientific, aspirations.[1] The unruliness of nature, its insubordination to laws, may now be understood in terms of that which is recognized as the essence of spirit.

But a spiritualistic metaphysics accounts for the regularities of nature as well as for its irregularities, or for just that degree of regularity which nature appears to have. For spirit is not disorderly, even though it is free. In the first place, it is directed toward the end which it pursues, and acquires thereby a steadiness and coherence which make it as predictable *as though it were* mechanically necessitated.[2] In the second place, as Ravaisson had said, it forms habits, or tends to "immobilize itself in any form which it once assumes." Although its acts are inaugurated by reason, they tend to become detached therefrom and to be propelled by one another. But habit (or mechanical nature), though a degraded state, is a state of spirit none the less.[3] Finally, it is only by the spiritualistic metaphysics that one can explain the fact that science, the creation of spirit, can fit the facts, and apply itself successfully to reality. We can explain this only if we suppose that there is a kinship between the human mind and nature, or that there is something of thought in nature, just as there is something of movement in mind.[4] Thus science,

---

[1] *Science et Religion*, p. 357.
[2] *De la Contingence*, etc., pp. 23, 70, 140.
[3] *Ibid.*, pp. 44, 162, 169, 170.
[4] *L'Idée de Loi naturelle*, pp. 19, 50, 133, 143.

instead of being opposed to spirit, appears as one of its creative activities; expressing, together with art and morality, that aspiration toward perfection which, as a community of wills and an organized, historic institution, constitutes religion.[1]

§ 16. Idealism in France. Renouvier. Lachelier

Spiritualism, both in Germany and in France, owed its force to the fact that it offered a positive account of reality. It transcended the relativities of phenomenal appearance not by affirming an opaque (unknown or material) underlying substance, but by depicting the inwardness of things luminously, as well as auspiciously, in terms of the intuition of spiritual activity. But in projecting this spiritual inwardness beyond phenomena and attributing it to nature and to God, it was necessary to make use of the argument from analogy. In the last analysis it was *interpretation*—plausible and meaningful, but highly speculative. The tendency from spiritualism to idealism expressed the desire to be more *rigorous*, or to carry over into the metaphysics of the nineteenth century the critical temper of the eighteenth, especially as exemplified by Kant.

In France this tendency found its most notable exponent in CHARLES RENOUVIER, who stood somewhat

---

[1] To the spiritualist school belong also Alfred FOUILLÉE (1838–1912; *La Liberté et le Déterminisme*, 1872; *L'Évolutionnisme des Idées-forces*, 1890), who sought to reconcile spiritualism and positivism through the conception of the tendency of ideas to realize themselves in action; and Jean Marie GUYAU (1854–1888; *Esquisse d'une Morale sans Obligation ni Sanction*, 1885), who took "life," or the will to live, as his ultimate and reconciling conception, thus anticipating Nietzsche and Bergson (§§ 22, 23).

apart from contemporary schools and currents of thought, as well as from academic circles, and struggled indefatigably during his long career to reconcile his moral and religious faith with his intellectual conscience. He did not limit himself to indubitable fact or intellectual certainty, but he sought scrupulously to define their limits, and to acknowledge explicitly the excursions he felt justified in making beyond them. The systematic works on which his fame chiefly rests were not published until he reached middle age. Born in 1815, his first period was spent in assimilating the philosophy of his age, especially that of Comte and Saint-Simon, and in mastering Descartes. His early publications expressed his historical interests together with a republican and socialistic enthusiasm inspired by the stirring events of 1848. His middle period, which coincided with the Second Empire and the defeat of his political hopes, was devoted to the writing and publication of his *Essais de Critique générale*, of which the first edition appeared in the years 1854–1869, and a second and revised edition in the years 1875–1886. This, his so-called "neo-criticism," was inspired by Kant. His last period, from 1886 until his death in 1903, was devoted to the restatement of his earlier doctrines, to the philosophy of history, and to the further development of his thought in the direction of a "personalistic" metaphysics.[1]

[1] The second edition of the *Essais de Critique générale* embraced a Treatise of General Logic (*Traité de Logique générale*, 3 vols.), a Treatise of Rational Psychology (*Traité de Psychologie rationelle*, 3 vols.), and *The Principles of Nature* (*Les Principes de la Nature*, 2 vols.). Among his other works the following are the most important: *Science de la Morale*, 2 vols., 1869; *Esquisse d'une Classification systématique des Doctrines*

That which sets Renouvier's philosophy apart from the spiritualistic metaphysics of his time, and relates him both to positivism and to idealism—both to Hume and to Kant, is his "phenomenism." Philosophy, like science, must eschew substances and begin with the appearances themselves. All that we immediately know (*connaître*) is the particular phenomenon—the "representation." This must not be construed at the outset as either inside or outside of ourselves, since it is prior to any such division of the world, and provides the datum in terms of which alone such a division can be justified. The representation does, however, possess a double character. It is both a "representing" and a "represented" (*representatif* and *representé*). These are the two inseparable aspects of the least unit of experience: it is an experience *of* something; and it is something *experienced*. Realism makes the mistake of supposing that objects can be divorced from the representation of them; idealism makes the mistake of supposing that there can be representation with nothing to represent.[1] These errors can be escaped only by taking experience, thus doubly qualified, to be self-sufficient and to constitute the very stuff of reality. The notion of a thing-in-itself or substance of things, divorced from this positive content, is utterly meaningless and vain. The true philosophy will be a "critique" of knowledge, which takes *experience* in the above sense as the sole

philosophiques, 2 vols., 1885–1886; *Philosophie analytique de l'Histoire*, 4 vols., 1896–1897; *La Nouvelle Monadologie*, 1899; *Les Dilemmes de la Métaphysique pure*, 1901; *Le Personnalisme*, 1903; and numerous articles in the reviews which he founded, the *Année philosophique* and the *Critique philosophique*.

[1] *Les Principes de la Nature*, edition of 1912, pp. 8–17

realm of fact, discovers the principles or categories which it involves, and by employing it as a norm, judges the legitimacy of the beliefs by which it is rounded into a metaphysics and philosophy of life.

Kant's error lay in his failure to construe the realm of experience in its own terms. He converted its two *aspects* into two realms lying outside it: the transcendental subject within and the transcendent object beyond. The effect is to make the knowable unreal and the real unknowable. It is true that provision must be made for a permanence and order of things (as distinguished from the individual's passing states), but this is to be found in the representations themselves. For representations have their own laws, or mutual relations of functional dependence. Over and above the particular laws or functions which the sciences discover, there are certain general laws which all representations obey, or which appertain to them generally *as representations*. These constitute the categories, of which Renouvier enumerated nine: relation, number, extent, duration, quality, becoming, causality, finality, and personality.[1] Of these the category of relation is the most abstract and universal, for to assert *anything* of a representation is to predicate a relation of it. This category is also the most objective, belonging to the representation as represented, rather than as representing. As we pass on there is a progression toward concreteness and subjectivity, the category of personality reflecting the fact that all representations are conscious; so that even when they are conceived by any consciousness as inde-

[1] Summarized in *Logique générale*, edition of 1912, vol. I, pp. 117–123.

pendent of itself, or as its "represented" rather than its "representing," they have to be conceived at the same time as representing something *to themselves,* or as having a personality of their own.

None of these categories, nor all of them together, permit of a total synthesis of the world.[1] They suffice for the limited purposes of science, but they carry us on from next to next, and never yield an absolute or whole. To pass beyond this relativity and indefiniteness of science we have to employ two deeper principles, the negative principle of contradiction and the positive principle of belief. Representations and their own immanent laws and categories give us knowledge of reality as far as they go, but they leave open the great issues or dilemmas of metaphysics, morality, and religion. Is the world infinite or finite? Is man free or determined? Is there or is there not a supreme moral order? The facts themselves yield no answer to these questions; and there is no escape from doubt unless we can find it by reflecting upon thought itself.

The principle of contradiction has to be accepted unless thought is to destroy itself. It proves a decisive consideration only in its application to the category of *number*. As distinct and multiple, representations can be counted; if they can be counted, then there is a number which corresponds to every multiplicity. But there is no infinite number. To avoid contradiction we must therefore suppose the world to be of finite extent in time and space; and to be composed of a finite number of indivisible units or monads. Kant's antinomies

[1] *Op. cit.,* vol. II, pp. 199–351.

are to be solved by accepting the thesis (finitude) and rejecting the antithesis (infinity) as contradictory.[1] God, if there be a God, must also be finite. Since there are first beginnings and discontinuities in the causal series, a place is made for freedom; not as Kant would have it, in some "noumenal" world, but in the world of fact and experience.

The metaphysical consequences of the principle of contradiction are largely negative and permissive. *Belief* is something more positive and more fundamental. For in order to apply even the principle of contradiction it is necessary first to believe or *accept* it. The same holds of the positive knowledge of science. This has a relatively high degree of certitude, and is *universally* accepted. But it has to be *accepted*, none the less, before it constitutes knowledge; and acceptance is an act of will. The truth does not force itself on us. Certainty is subjective; it means that we evaluate evidence, cease to think further, and come to a decision. Thus the ground is shifted from the general considerations of logic and experience to an analysis of man, with special reference to the relation of cognition and will.[2]

Will is not a force operating *ab extra* on representations, but consists in the character which representations themselves have of maintaining themselves in consciousness. That they should derive this power from within themselves is entirely conceivable, once it is admitted that there *are* absolute beginnings in nature. When so construed as the tendency of a repre-

---

[1] *Logique générale*, edition of 1912, pp. 214–221.
[2] Cf. the *Psychologie rationelle, passim.*

sentation to maintain itself, and when in exclusive possession of consciousness to be followed by the appropriate movements, the will does not differ essentially from belief, which is committal to a representation, or affirmation of it, as distinguished from doubt or the prolongation of reflection.

The distinction between truth and error would mean nothing unless it were supposed that the will could choose freely in accordance with the evidence. If truth consisted in believing what one could not help believing, then necessary error would be truth. The love of truth implies the *search* for evidence, as distinguished from hasty and careless belief. But this implies a freedom to believe when one wills, or when one ought. Freedom itself cannot be proved beyond doubt, but has to be freely believed. Freedom is thus a postulate of knowledge, but it is also, as Kant had contended, a postulate of morality. Indeed, to conceive knowledge as belief, freely adopted by the will, is to recognize that knowledge and morality are indivisible. From this position the transition is easily made to a doctrine of immortality and of God, justified on moral grounds.

Although Renouvier thus traces belief to will, he does not in the least suppose it to be a matter of caprice. Justifiable belief is that which satisfies the demands of the *total personality*.[1] These demands qualify one another: will is as much bound to satisfy the intellect, as intellect to satisfy will. There is a coherent demand which constitutes the ultimate standard of "reasonableness." And man is entitled to demand that the uni-

[1] Cf. *Esquisse d'une Classification*, etc., vol. II, ch. 3 and *passim*.

verse shall satisfy *his* demands only in so far as he on his side accepts the demands of the universe, as revealed in his moral nature. There is a sort of fundamental compact between man and the universe, according to which the universe engages itself to correspond with the requirements of righteousness.[1]

Renouvier's philosophy represents the attempt to construct a world out of phenomena and their laws. The phenomenon, the given fact of experience, is qualified to exist, as it is. It is true that there are ultimate metaphysical questions which can be answered only in terms of unverifiable beliefs, and which take us beyond the limits of actual phenomena, but this is not because there is anything inherently unreal in the phenomenon as such. Instead of being, as the term "phenomenon" suggests, the mere appearance *of* something *to* the mind, it takes up these two modes of reference into itself as its own aspects. Thus Renouvier may be said to have converted criticism into a metaphysics, or to have converted appearance into reality by removing its disparaging implications. This view is to be contrasted with agnosticism, which conceives reality to lie inaccessibly behind phenomena; with dogmatism or eclecticism, which supposes that this reality beyond phenomena can be brought into view by the peculiar rays of the intellect; and with intuitionism, which supposes that it may be interpreted by analogy in terms of the subject's direct acquaintance with himself as a free,

---

[1] The most important of the followers of Renouvier (excepting James, § 24) was Octave HAMELIN (1856–1907; *Essais sur les Éléments principaux de la Représentation*, 1907), who adopted a position close to that of Hegel.

SPIRITUALISM AND IDEALISM

voluntary activity. There is a fourth alternative to Renouvier's phenomenism, which in German thought appeared in the Hegelian interpretation of Kant, and in French thought in the philosophy of Lachelier. According to this view phenomena are construed not as the appearance of something to something, but as *products of thought*. The metaphysical reality is then creative thought, together with the inherent principles which govern its activity.

JULES LACHELIER (1832–1918), like Ravaisson, has an importance in French philosophy out of proportion to the extent of his written works. Of these there are only two of importance, the doctoral dissertation on *The Foundation of Induction*[1] and the article on *Psychology and Metaphysics*. With the conciseness and rigor of thought which characterized his writings were united remarkable personal qualities, through which he exerted a powerful influence both on his students at the École Supérieure, where he taught from 1864 to 1875, and on his colleagues and friends during the years of his service as Inspecteur de l'Académie de Paris and Inspecteur Général de l'Instruction Publique, and during the later years of his retirement.

Lachelier diverged from the prevailing French spiritualism both in demanding rigorous proofs in place of intuition and analogy, and in construing spirit in terms of thought rather than of will. These two points are

[1] *Du Fondement de l'Induction*, 1871. This, together with the *Psychologie et Métaphysique* (which originally appeared in 1885, in the *Revue de Métaphysique et de Morale*), and (in later editions) the *Notes sur le Pari de Pascal*, appeared in a single volume in 1896.

closely connected, since the alleged datum of inner intuition is will, while spirit, *argued as a necessity*, assumes the form of thought. Lachelier's point of departure was the Kantian view (which Lachelier accepted as against Hume) that the empirical world of science derives its organization from the mind, and the universality of its laws from the fact that, being the product of the mind, it cannot fail to agree with the mind's constitution. As with Kant, the categories are essentially modes of synthesis by which thought constructs its world. Lachelier went beyond Kant, however, in affirming that the world of organized experience, instead of representing an adjustment of thought to externally given data, is through and through the product of thought; determined wholly by the inner requirements of thought, and revealing thought as the only substantive reality.

Lachelier's persistent effort to deduce the world from thought is divisible into three main arguments: first, the world may be shown to be *congruent* with thought; second, the world can be *explained* only by supposing it to be produced by thought; third, thought *does* produce the world through a creative activity whose *modus operandi* can be demonstrated.

Nature as a mechanical system, where all is in movement under necessary law, satisfies the intellectual demand for unity. Mechanism, in itself, however, does not imply that anything shall actually happen or exist, only that A shall occur if B occurs. There is an aspect of will allied to the purely intellectual aspect of thought, and this requires a concrete world of things and events. In order to reconcile this reality with the requirements of unity it is necessary to introduce the category of finality, for realities determine one another not mechanically but as means to ends or as parts of one whole. Mechanism is thus degraded to an abstract and symbolic representation of the deeper and more concrete principle of finality.

The world thus constituted does actually satisfy the demands of thought, or is thinkable. But how do we know that this is not an effect of reality upon thought, or a mere happy accident? Thought is itself real (rather than merely an echo or reflection of reality) only provided it creates its world, and does not merely discover and analyze it. Addressing himself to this question, in his *Psychology and Metaphysics*, Lachelier here attacked that traditional French psychology which would reduce the psychical to the physiological and physical. He argued that continuous physical *extension*, for example, is explicable only in terms of an act of perception which first "posits" a whole and then explores its interior; and that the *externality* of the physical world is explicable only in terms of the antithesis between the sense quality, on the one hand, and feeling or motor reaction on the other. But, most important of all, physical and psychical facts alike are freed from relativity and given objectivity only by belonging to a system of *truths*, which are judged and predicted by thought. If the world is thus explicable only by thought, then the existence of the world proves the existence of thought.

But Lachelier was not content to base the existence of thought on anything so dubious as the existent world: he attempted by a bold use of the dialectical method to establish the reality of thought independently, and to evolve the existent world out of it.[1] Thought begins with the idea of *being*, a truth which proves itself, since to doubt it is to affirm that it *is* true that it either is or is not. But thought is not content with this condition of mere abstract being. In order to think itself as a something which *has* being, as an attribute, it invokes sensibility, which gives a material content to space and time. This step is not deducible from abstract being, but is an act of will, in which thought shows itself to be something more than pure intellect. The last and highest stage is that of self-conscious reflection, in which thought distinguishes itself as pure act or freedom from objects projected outside itself.

This may be expressed by saying that thought appears on three levels. First, the idea of abstract being or truth, because of its peculiarly recurrent character, takes on the symbolic or external forms of time and linear space conceived as series of homogeneous units, and of mechanical causality conceived as abstract or hypothetical possibility in time and space. Second, the thought of something in particular, not being deducible from abstract being, involves an act of positing or will, and is externalized in the visible two-dimensional field of space, with a content provided by sensation, and determined by final causality. Third, the thought of itself as the original act and source externalizes itself in the third and invisible dimension of nature, in spatial depth, in the distinction between the near and remote and in the sphere of action. Thus thought is,

[1] *Psychologie et Métaphysique*, edition of 1924, pp. 158 ff.

first, intellectual and abstract and mechanical; second, desiderative, pictorial, concrete, and teleological; third, active and real. The last word is liberty, but it is the liberty of thought to think, and in thinking to express its own nature and create a world.

These three levels of thought also signify to Lachelier the progression from science to art, and from art to religion. The mechanical system of science is complete in its own terms, and permits of no exceptions. But thought can rise to a higher view, in which the world assumes the form of realized and harmonious ends. Finally, in morality thought achieves the higher level of freedom. But since freedom attaches to *thought,* and since thought is *universal,* morality passes over into religion, in which the individual recognizes his dependence on the universal thought, or God. Being a disillusioned republican, Lachelier justified political absolutism as the reign of the impersonal ideal or will of God; while as a Catholic he found in humility and faith a way of rising above the intellectual formulas of philosophy to an immediate sense of the concrete reality of the divine life.[1]

---

[1] Contemporary French idealism tends toward a critical examination of the categories of science, after the manner of neo-Kantianism, but with explicit reference to recent developments in mathematics and physics. LÉON BRUNSCHVICG contends that the categories or principles of thinking mind cannot be deduced, but must be traced through their actual operation in the history of science. The nature of reason is revealed only in its application to the facts of experience. Cf. his *Étapes de la Philosophie mathématique,* 1912; and *L'Expérience humaine et la Causalité physique,* 1922.

É. MEYERSON, who is less closely identified with this philosophical tradition, finds in science a similar duality between the unity and identity which are sought by reason and the irreducible novelty, movement, and temporality of existence. Cf. his *Identité et Réalité,* 1908, and *La Déduction relativiste,* 1925.

§ 17. Idealism in England. Green. Bradley. Bosanquet

In England it was idealism rather than spiritualism which was the champion of the moral and religious tradition against the naturalistic tendencies of the middle of the last century. The Kantian and post-Kantian doctrines, first unqualifiedly adopted by Stirling,[1] found their most influential exponent among English philosophers in THOMAS HILL GREEN. He was born in 1836, and his career was identified with Oxford University, where he was first an undergraduate, afterward a fellow and tutor of Balliol College, and finally, from 1878 until his death in 1882, professor of moral philosophy. His most important works were originally delivered in the form of lectures, and the power exerted by his teaching was as far-reaching as that exerted by his writings. He was the accepted leader of the reaction against the cult of Buckle, Darwin, and Spencer; but in combating naturalism he went back to its roots in empiricism, and thus repudiated the whole British philosophical tradition, the essential errors of which he believed to be most perfectly exemplified in the work of Hume. Indeed, the only expression of his views which was published during his life consisted in Introductions appended to an edition of Hume's *Treatises*.[2] But Green was not less interested in combating the utilitarian moral philosophy, which he believed to be as untenable as the

---

[1] § 4.
[2] *A Treatise on Human Nature*, by David Hume, edited by T. H. Green and T. H. Grose, 2 vols., 1874. The *Prolegomena to Ethics* appeared in 1883, and the *Works*, 3 vols. (including his important *Principles of Political Obligation* and miscellaneous historical writings), in the years 1885–1888.

empiricism in which it was rooted; and the most systematic and important of his works, in which he derived the principle of self-realization from an idealistic theory of knowledge, bears the title of *Prolegomena to Ethics.*

Green took as his point of departure "that analysis of the conditions of knowledge which forms the basis of all Critical Philosophy, whether called by the name of Kant or no." The beginning of knowledge is "the experience of connected matters of fact." Empiricism (as exemplified by Hume) makes the mistake of supposing that the "connection" can itself be one of the matters of fact,[1] whereas it has to be supplied by thought. The Kantian forms and categories become for Green the *connective* tissue of the known world. Sensation or "feeling" supplies the terms, but thought alone can supply the relations. There cannot even be a succession of feelings unless there subsists between them a relation which is not a feeling, and which is not itself in the line of succession. Things do not unite *themselves* into a relation, but require the intervention *ab extra* of some "combining agency." Since nothing can enter into knowledge that is unrelated to consciousness, this combining agency must be an activity of consciousness. "With such a combining agency we are familiar as our intelligence," our "thinking or self-distinguishing consciousness."[2] The unity of nature is explicable only as an expression of the unity of the self.

But Green would not have us suppose that this explanation of nature in terms of our "combining intelli-

[1] *Prolegomena,* § 8. [2] *Ibid.,* §§ 28, 10, 29, 46.

gence" is, as Kant thought, prejudicial to its reality. This would be so, if, in the first place, there were another reality which lay beyond this combining intelligence, whether of things-in-themselves, or of bare sensations produced by things-in-themselves. Sensations are nothing, according to Green, except in so far as they are brought into systematic relations, and their dependence on things-in-themselves could mean nothing except in terms of such relations extended illegitimately beyond experience. To know anything, whether sensations or things-in-themselves, is to relate; and to relate is to confer on the terms related whatever meaning, reality, and "objectivity" they possess.

The product of a relating consciousness would be unreal, in the second place, if it were the work of the private, individual mind, with its own particular and limited field of experience—with its place in nature and its moment in history. We must suppose, therefore, that the combining intelligence which creates the real system of nature, as distinguished from that of our private and limited selves, is an "eternal intelligence," which determines nature in advance of our individual human acquaintance with it, and "partially and gradually reproduces itself in us." [1] This divine mind, which constitutes the universal system of reality, is not itself subject to any of the relational categories which it produces; and if we speak of it as a "cause," we must understand this term in the unique sense of that free and spontaneous activity with which we are acquainted in our own thought.[2]

[1] *Prolegomena*, §§ 36 ff.   [2] *Ibid.*, § 78.

Because man can *know*, or participate in that "combining intelligence" which constitutes nature, he cannot be himself merely a part of nature. But man transcends nature not only cognitively in respect of his intelligence, but also morally in respect of his will. To understand will it is first necessary to understand desire, which is distinguished from mere instinct through being self-conscious; and from intellect, in that while the latter gives ideality to an apparently alien material, desire gives material content or reality to what is at first only an ideal.[1] Will is distinguishable from *mere* desire not as the strongest desire, but as that desire with which the agent *identifies himself*.[2] Thus all voluntary action is directed to the end of realizing a certain idea of one's self. The object of desire or will is *ipso facto* good, in the generic sense; but it is *morally* good only when it is the object of a *moral* will.[3]

What, then, is this moral will which is in each one of us? The answer is to be found again in the implication of an eternal mind, which "reproduces" itself in man as that aspiration to perfection or to the absolutely best, which is characteristic of our moral consciousness.[4] The moral will is the willing by man of God's will.

But how does man know the divine will? For answer, Green had to employ the assumption that history and organized society are its embodiments. The state, which is an expression of will rather than of force, owes its authority to its being the expression of a "collective will."[5] Thus Green, although he did not adopt the dia-

---

[1] *Prolegomena*, §§ 130–133. [2] *Ibid.*, § 143. [3] *Ibid.*, § 171.
[4] *Ibid.*, §§ 173, 174. [5] *Principles of Moral Obligation*, *passim*.

lectical method of Hegel, and was both nationally and temperamentally inclined to individualism, found himself forced by the exigencies of his philosophical premises toward the universalism and authoritarianism which had been the characteristic developments of the classic idealism in Germany.[1]

FRANCIS HERBERT BRADLEY (1846–1924), like Green, who was his teacher, waged war on contemporary naturalism, and on the British empirical and utilitarian tradition. Like Green, he drew his inspiration from Kantian sources, and in particular from Hegel. Otherwise there is a marked contrast between these leaders of the British idealistic movement. Although resident at Oxford, Bradley was prevented by ill-health from assuming the duties of an academic career, and spent the greater part of his life in seclusion, as a research fellow of Merton College. Profiting by his leisure and despite his ill-health, Bradley, unlike Green, developed his views systematically, and defended them against attack. His first book, entitled *Ethical Studies* (1876), was both a critique of hedonism, and a development of the thesis that the good lies in the realization of a harmonious and unified self in organic relations with society. In *The Principles of Logic* (1883)[2] he developed two important theses. As against the psychological

---

[1] A closer approach to the position of Hegel is to be found in the Cairds. EDWARD CAIRD (1835–1908) is notable for his personal influence as Master of Balliol College, and for his *Critical Account of the Philosophy of Kant* (1877); JOHN CAIRD (1820–1898), for his *Introduction to the Philosophy of Religion* (1880).

[2] Two vols., second edition published in 1914.

method he asserted that the subject of judgment is not an idea, but is *reality*, which is qualified by the total ideal content of the judgment. Thus judgment takes us at once beyond the judging mind, and so beyond the jurisdiction of psychology. As against empiricism, he asserted that the act of judgment, instead of being a reproduction of data given in sense-perception, is grounded in ulterior *judgments* as part of a coherent and rational system of thought.

The *Appearance and Reality*, which was published in 1891,[1] revealed most clearly the qualities of Bradley's mind. An acute dialectician, and committed to the thesis that the real is the rational, he here turned the intellect against itself and held the traditional idealistic categories—especially that category of relation which Green had accepted as fundamental—to be contradictory and untenable. Although more intellectualistic than Green in his method, he found his ultimate solution in immediacy and feeling. In the controversy stimulated by this famous work, Bradley took an active part through a series of articles, many of which were brought together in the last of his books, *Truth and Reality*, which was published in 1914.

The root of Bradley's metaphysics and theory of knowledge lies in the distinction already alluded to, between reality as the subject of judgment, and the ideal content which judgment ascribes to it; or the distinction between the "that" and the "what." Reality is somehow indicated in experience as *that* which we think about; but reality is also *what* we think about it.

[1] Second enlarged edition, 1897.

That we should be compelled to think about it, and hold it to be what we think, proves that it is not real as it is given. Thought is the effort to supplement the evident inadequacy of immediate experience, by introducing distinctions and qualifications both within and without. But thought finds it impossible to complete this task. Its affirmations always point beyond themselves, so that as soon as they are made they have to be denied. There is no escape from the difficulty. We can neither accept experience without thinking it, nor can we think it successfully; thought is both necessary and self-contradictory. This characteristic pervades all of the categories, but is seen most clearly in the fundamental categories of substantive, adjective, quality, and relation.

We employ the categories of *substantive* and *adjective* when we say, of any given thing M, that M is a. But either M and a are the same, in which case we have said nothing; or they are different, in which case we have contradicted ourselves in saying that M is a. If, on the other hand, we mean that M is a, but not *merely* a, because of being also b, then we have to ask how M can be both a and b if a and b are different. Either we again contradict ourselves, or we have destroyed the unity of M, and put two things, a and b, in its place. We may seek to evade these contradictions by substituting for the inherence of the adjectives a and b, in the substantive M, a direct relation between the qualities a and b, as when the empiricist reduces a thing to the sum of its properties. But we now encounter fresh difficulties, in the category of *relation*. Either we have

SPIRITUALISM AND IDEALISM

to treat the relation to b as an adjective of a and the relation to a as an adjective of b—in which case the old difficulties reappear, and are aggravated by the supposition that a and b can be *reciprocally* substantive and adjective—or we have to treat the relation itself (r) as a third being, which merely increases the multiplicity without achieving any unity. For if our only unifying principle is relation, we have now to relate r to a and to b by new relations r^1 and r^2, and so on *ad infinitum*.[1]

By a similar method Bradley disposes of the traditional conceptions of primary and secondary qualities, space and time, motion and change, causation, activity, self, and things-in-themselves, and thus by implication refutes materialism, phenomenalism, agnosticism, and monadic spiritualism.

But although this critique discredits most of the categories of common-sense and of philosophy, and compels us to relegate them to "appearance" as distinguished from reality, the results are by no means wholly negative. In the first place, we have discovered a *criterion*. "Ultimate reality is such that it does not contradict itself";[2] it must be self-consistent. Secondly, it must contain the appearances, for there is no other disposition that can be made of these. Combining these two affirmations we conclude that in reality appearance must be "concordant and other than it seems." Thirdly, reality must be one, for whether we perceive them together or think them together, different reals must *qualify* one

---

[1] *Appearance and Reality*, chs. II, III. Cf. also *Truth and Reality*, ch. VIII.
[2] *Appearance and Reality*, edition of 1908, p. 136.

another; and in accordance with the fundamental criterion they must be supposed to qualify one another as parts of a *harmonious whole*.[1] Fourthly, reality is sentient experience. "There is no being or fact outside of that which is commonly called psychical existence." [2] It follows from all of these conclusions that reality is an individual experience in which all appearances are harmoniously resolved. This reality is henceforth referred to as the Absolute.

The Absolute is, however, not a mere construction. We cannot, it is true, enter into the Absolute's experience, but its "main features" are within our own. "Complex wholes are felt as single experiences." Mere feeling or "immediate presentation" is the experience of a whole containing diversity "not parted by relations"; it fails to satisfy us only because of its incompleteness.[3] We never see reality, so to speak, "but through a hole." [4] We attempt to complete it "by relational addition from without and by relational distinction from within." On this level our experience is self-contradictory. But we can form the idea of a "positive non-relational non-objective whole of feeling," [5] that shall be above this level rather than below it—"a whole become immediate at a higher stage without losing any richness," in which the diversity brought

---

[1] *Appearance and Reality*, edition of 1908, pp. 140–143.
[2] *Ibid.*, p. 144. Cf. *Truth and Reality*, p. 315. This does not mean, Bradley points out, that reality is subjective, for the conception of sentient experience is prior to the distinction between subject and object.
[3] *Appearance and Reality.*, edition of 1908, pp. 159, 521.
[4] *Principles of Logic*, Book I, ch. II, § 29.
[5] *Truth and Reality*, pp. 188–189.

SPIRITUALISM AND IDEALISM 135

to light on the relational level shall be "merged" but preserved.[1]

Furthermore, this process of advancing to higher immediacies through intermediate stages of discursive thought is known to us in our æsthetic, cognitive, and moral experiences. From the standpoint of the higher levels the lower levels are seen to be partial "appearances" or "degrees" of the same reality. Thus "truth and life, beauty and goodness" are all revelations of an Absolute which must be all that *they* are, and yet pass beyond the defects which mar even these reconciling harmonies. No appearances fall outside the Absolute, and all must, in the Absolute, be in some measure other than they appear, in order that their contradictions may be overcome; but while some will undergo a "rearrangement" so radical as to be unrecognizable, others, which we commonly call "higher," afford us genuine premonitions of the Absolute perfection.

After Green and Bradley the most important member of the British idealistic school was BERNARD BOSANQUET.[2] Like Bradley and his idealistic predecessors, Bosanquet identifies the existent world with the con-

---

[1] *Appearance and Reality*, edition of 1908, pp. 160, 241-242.

[2] 1848-1923. Author of *Logic*, 1888; *History of Æsthetic*, 1892; *Philosophical Theory of the State*, 1899; *The Principle of Individuality and Value*, 1912; *The Value and Destiny of the Individual*, 1913; and numerous other works. Bosanquet's successor in this line of thought is R. F. A. Hoernlé (1880- ; *Studies in Contemporary Metaphysics*, 1920; *Matter, Life, Mind and God*, 1922). Other British idealists of the same idealistic tradition are J. S. Mackenzie (1860- ; *Outlines of Metaphysics*, 1902; *Elements of Constructive Philosophy*, 1917), J. H. Muirhead (1855- ; *Elements of Ethics*, 1892; *Social Purpose*, 1918), and A. E. Taylor (1869- ; *Elements of Metaphysics*, 1903).

tent of rationalized experience. He differed from Bradley in that he emphasized the success of thought (in reconciling immediacy and logic) rather than its failures. His leading idea was the *concrete universal*, revealed in the higher synthetic experiences, and in the "collective will," [1] the latter furnishing the basis for his political and social teachings. His philosophy, which is rich in incidental insight, may be taken as proclaiming the idea of wholeness, as furnishing the key to logic, metaphysics, ethics, art, and religion. Truth lies in systematic coherence; reality in the all-embracing individual whole, of which the parts possess degrees of reality in proportion as they mirror the whole; moral and political action should be governed by the will of the whole; and it is the whole, as revealed in its parts, which is the proper object both of æsthetic contemplation and of religious reverence.

§ 18. Idealism in America. Royce. Howison. Bowne

The idealism of JOSIAH ROYCE differed profoundly from that of Green and Bradley. Born in California, when that State was still a remote frontier community; influenced in his early youth by the evolutionary teachings of Le Conte,[2] and by his studies of Mill and Spencer; afterward intimately associated with James,[3] his thought always retained a naturalistic and empirical flavor. As an American he was predisposed to individualism, and sought earnestly to reconcile this motive with the absolutistic trend of his philosophy. He acquired a strong interest in symbolic logic and the philos-

---

[1] Cf. Green, above.   [2] § 5.   [3] § 25.

ophy of mathematics, and employed them in his conception of the infinite and in his studies of methodology. Finally, he was led through his early religious training and his social interests to attempt a philosophical interpretation of Christianity. Nevertheless the influences which most profoundly moulded his thought were those received in Germany from his studies of Lotze, Schopenhauer, Kant, and Schelling. Romanticism made a strong appeal to him because of his interest in literature and music, and it is this influence which is most clearly reflected in his first book, *The Religious Aspect of Philosophy*, published in 1885. His most important work was *The World and the Individual* (1900–1901), which reveals a profound study of Hegel, of Indian philosophy, and of scholasticism.[1] He taught philosophy at Harvard University from 1882 until his death in 1916.

Whereas for Bradley immediate experience proves unsatisfactory and evokes thought to piece it out, for Royce it is thought which seeks to complete itself in immediate experience. With Bradley reality is a datum, given inadequately in finite experience and adequately in the Absolute, with conceptual thinking as a transition from the one level to the other. With Royce, on the other hand, reality is essentially the object of thought; so that whereas for Bradley thinking may be regarded as infected with contradiction, because it is transcended in reality, for Royce it must be acquitted of the charge and its good name restored.

[1] The more important of his other writings were: *The Spirit of Modern Philosophy*, 1892; *The Conception of God* (in collaboration with Le Conte, Howison, and S. E. Mezes), 1897; *The Philosophy of Loyalty*, 1908; *The Problem of Christianity* (2 vols.), 1913.

Starting (after the manner of British empiricism) with "finite ideas," Royce finds that they possess an "internal" and an "external" meaning.[1] Over and above its content, the judging thought carries a reference beyond itself to its object. This object cannot be regarded as an "independent real," for then it could never be known; nor as a mystical immediacy which "quenches" thought, for then it would be unintelligible; nor as a possibility of experience determined by valid ideas, for a *mere* possibility is nothing at all. Realism, mysticism, and "critical rationalism" being thus disposed of, idealism is introduced as the view which defines reality as the *fulfilment of ideas*, in which the purpose embodied in their internal meaning is realized in the experience of their external meaning. Only the idea itself can recognize its own object, as that which it intended, and thus testify authoritatively to its own fulfilment. The object can be "individual" only when the idea chooses it, claims it, and refuses otherwise to be satisfied.[2] Both the specificity of objective reference and the uniqueness of particular facts depend on thus construing ideas as having wills of their own. Thought is a conscious "life," in which ideas find satisfaction in their objects. "To be, in the final sense, means to be just such a life, complete, present to experience, and conclusive of the search for perfection which every finite idea in its own measure undertakes when it seeks for any object." [3]

---

[1] *World and the Individual*, vol. I, Lect. VII.
[2] *Conception of God*, pp. 217–272.
[3] *World and the Individual*, vol. I, pp. 341–342.

SPIRITUALISM AND IDEALISM

The Absolute appears in Royce's philosophy in response to two demands. In the first place, reality must fulfil *all* ideas. In order to escape the relativity and conflict of finite ideas, it is necessary to suppose that they are taken up into one self-consistent system of ideas, or one individual purpose and will, which finds its satisfaction in the total realm of existence. In the second place, there can be no facts that are not experienced; and the Absolute experience is thus invoked to provide for such facts as are implied in finite experience, but fall outside it. The very possibility of truth and error, which attaches to all finite ideas, compels us to assume that there is a more inclusive experience which comprehends both the purposes of finite ideas and also the facts in which these purposes are fulfilled or thwarted.[1]

Royce recognized that the conception of the Absolute involved a logical difficulty and he resolutely faced it. If the Absolute experiences all facts, then this is in turn a fact which the Absolute must experience, and so on *ad infinitum*. The Absolute is, therefore, both a unity and at the same time an endless series of self-representations. It must, in other words, be a completed infinite. But in the light of modern mathematics this is no longer a self-contradiction. It is true that the infinite cannot be exhausted by enumeration, and has no last term, but it can be defined *positively* as a system which is similar (in the sense of one to one correspondence) to a part of itself. The Absolute knows itself as infinite, or so defines itself as to provide at one stroke

[1] *Religious Aspect of Philosophy*, ch. XI.

(*totum simul*) for a richness of content which, because known to be inexhaustible, it does not vainly seek to exhaust.[1]

With this monistic metaphysics Royce sought earnestly to reconcile the distinctive peculiarities of human experience. He was not satisfied to declare them to be mere appearances, but sought to provide for them in reality. Thus time is not an unreality to be superseded by the eternal, but is a peculiar sequence which in the Absolute is grasped all at once, as human perception grasps a melody.[2] Evil is not transmuted into good, and therefore condoned, but remains as that which even in the Absolute has to be resisted and overcome.[3] Human individuals are not swallowed up in the Absolute, but each is a unique part of the unique whole, contributing through its own expression of the divine will something which is both indispensable to the whole and peculiar to itself.[4]

Royce's thought tended to a greater and greater emphasis on the conception of society. In his theory of knowledge he came to define thought in terms of "interpretation," rather than in terms of the meaning of ideas. The latter was a direct relation of idea and object; the former is a social relation, in which one mind's idea becomes a sign of the object to a second mind.[5] His ethics centred in the principle of "loyalty," or of the individual's devotion to a "cause" greater than

---

[1] *World and the Individual*, vol. I, Supplementary Essay.
[2] *Ibid.*, vol. II, Lect. III.
[3] *Religious Aspect of Philosophy*, pp. 452, 465.
[4] *Conception of God*, pp. 272–275.
[5] *Problem of Christianity*, vol. II, Lects. XIII, XIV.

himself. The ultimate moral principle is that of "loyalty to loyalty" in which the individual, while serving his own cause, respects and co-operates with the spirit of loyalty wherever he finds it. It was this spirit to which Royce looked for a solution of racial and international problems through the idea of "The Great Community." [1] Finally, he found the essence of Christianity to consist in a "community of the faithful," "hopefully and practically devoted to the cause of the still invisible, but perfectly real and divine Universal Community." [2]

The tendency which was so marked in Royce's philosophy, to emphasize the human individual and to conceive values in terms of society, found a bolder expression in the "personal idealism" of GEORGE H. HOWISON (1825–1916), who as professor at the University of California from 1884 until 1909 exerted a notable influence upon the cultural development of the Pacific Coast. In a public discussion with Royce and others, held at the University of California in 1895,[3] Howison attacked Royce's "Monistic Idealism," or conception of the Absolute, and defended a *"Pluralistic Idealism,"* on the ground that an "Infinite Inclusive Self" would not only swallow up and annihilate all human selves, but lose its own selfhood; since selfhood is essentially a *moral* consciousness, implying the recognition of *other* selves.

---

[1] *Philosophy of Loyalty*, and *The Hope of the Great Community* (1916).
[2] *Problem of Christianity*, vol. II, p. 425.
[3] This discussion was published in 1897, under the title of *The Conception of God* (cf. p. 547, note 3).

In a later book, entitled *The Limits of Evolution*,[1] Howison developed this thesis more systematically, against monism both of the naturalistic type, as exemplified by Spencer and Haeckel, and of the idealistic type, as exemplified by the Hegelian school. Having refuted naturalism on Kantian grounds, Howison's main purpose was to save Kantianism from destroying itself through the internal conflict between its cognitive and its practical principles. Nature is the product of the cognitive mind, and the systematic unity of nature suggests that it is the product of *one absolute* mind, of which the human mind is only a mode or vehicle. The practical or moral consciousness, on the other hand, implies that the human individual is one of a circle or kingdom of free, immortal, and autonomous persons. How reconcile these counter-claims of universality and personality? Only, thinks Howison, by construing cognition in terms of a "social logic," in which objectivity and truth are held to consist in a "universal social recognition."[2] Nature is the creation of our several personal selves, but nature is one, because we are like-minded and guided by the same rational purpose.

This unifying purpose finds its supreme expression in God. As a reality, God is one person among others. Only by recognizing persons other than himself who have rights, and toward whom he has duties, can God be a moral person at all. He does not include human individuals within himself, nor does he coerce them,

---

[1] The full title was *The Limits of Evolution and Other Essays Illustrating the Metaphysical Theory of Personal Idealism*, 1901; 2d and revised edition, 1904.

[2] *Op. cit.*, edition of 1904, pp. xxxvi–xxxviii.

SPIRITUALISM AND IDEALISM

but he acts upon them by attraction (by "final" or "moral" causation), as the *ideal* which they adopt of their own free will.[1] The realm of nature, or the world of sense, also falls outside of God, as being the product of the human mind. So God is not responsible for evil, but may be worshipped as the embodiment of perfection. He is the "Supreme Instance" in the "eternal circle of Persons," the first "citizen" in "the all-founding, all-governing Realm of Spirits."[2]

"Personal" idealism manifests three characteristic tendencies. In the first place, it tends, through its desire to save the individual and his moral attributes, to emphasize the will and the practical consciousness, at the expense of the theoretical reason. Although Howison himself resisted this tendency, it resulted among British idealists in a movement toward voluntarism and pragmatism.[3] In the second place, personal idealism tends to an emphasis on *society* as a means of saving itself from the relativistic and sceptical consequences of an unqualified individualism. Finally, personal ideal-

---

[1] *Limits of Evolution*, pp. 65, 328.
[2] *Ibid.*, p. 355; *Conception of God*, p. 113.
[3] That is, toward the type of philosophy discussed below, Part IV. This transition in British thought is exemplified by the volume of essays entitled *Personal Idealism*, which appeared in 1902, and in which idealists, voluntarists, and pragmatists united on the common ground of pluralism. Exponents of the same "personalistic" tendency, but standing nearer to the centre of idealism, are Thomas Davidson (1840–1900), in America; and in England, James Ward (1843–1925; *Naturalism and Agnosticism*, 1899; *The Realm of Ends*, 1911), J. M. E. McTaggart (1866–1925; *Studies in Hegelian Cosmology*, 1901; *Some Dogmas of Religion*, 1906; *The Nature of Existence*, 1921), and A. Seth Pringle-Pattison (1856– ; *Hegelianism and Personality*, 1887; *Man's Place in the Cosmos*, 1897; *The Idea of God in the Light of Modern Philosophy*, 1917).

ism tends to emphasize the substantive reality of persons, as known immediately in self-consciousness, and thus moves toward a spiritualism of the Lotzean type. The most influential exponent in America of this last tendency was BORDEN PARKER BOWNE.[1] This philosopher's interests were primarily metaphysical and religious. As for his teacher Lotze, so for Bowne, the real is that which can act and be acted upon, of which spirit is the only known case. The real meaning of the categories is to be found not in their conceptual or formal rôle, as modes of connection among phenomena, but "through our living experience of intelligence itself." In this "active self-experience" is to be found a revelation of causality, of substance, of unity-in-manyness, and of identity in change. The categories so construed in terms of the real mind which creates phenomena, may then be assigned to the reality beyond phenomena—a step which all philosophers have virtually taken in acknowledging the reality of other selves. This doctrine Bowne called his "transcendental empiricism."

The speculative reason recognizes its own limits, and beyond these "we have to fall back on belief based on the necessities or the intimations of practical life."[2] This principle of faith Bowne employed to justify the hopeful bias and the specific dogmas of religion, recognizing as did Lotze and Ritschl that these dogmas need to be variously expressed and perpetually restated, in

[1] 1847–1910. His most important writings were *Studies in Theism*, 1879; and *Metaphysics*, 1882 (2d edition, 1898). A brief popular summary of his position was contained in *Personalism*, 1908.
[2] *Metaphysics* (1898), p. 427.

order that they may preserve their value in terms of the living religious experience. But the speculative reason lays the foundation of religion in a spiritualistic metaphysics, which defines "a world of persons with a Supreme Person at the head," of which nature is the expression and means of communication, and which, despite their ultimate substantial and causal unity, nevertheless as persons preserve a "mutual otherness" and "relative independence." [1]

§ 19. Critical Idealism in Germany. Cohen. Natorp

The revival of Kant in Germany in the 1860's was followed by a revival of those very post-Kantian tendencies against which the Kantian revival had itself protested. Although neo-Kantianism sprang from a desire to purge Kantianism of the alien elements introduced by Hegel, Fichte, and Romanticism, it was promptly followed by neo-Hegelianism, neo-Fichteanism, and neo-Romanticism. There appears, in other words, to be an inevitable and recurrent cycle through which the thought of Kant passes, inspired by the in-

---

[1] *Metaphysics*, part I, ch. II; *Personalism*, p. 277. Next after those mentioned in the text, the most prominent of American idealists at the opening of the century was James E. Creighton (1861–1924; *Studies in Speculative Philosophy*, 1925), for many years an influential teacher at Cornell University. The American idealist who follows Royce most closely is Mary W. Calkins (*The Persistent Problems of Philosophy*, 1907; *The Good Man and the Good*, 1918). Another thinker whose position is close to that of Royce is W. E. Hocking, who argues that "nature is always present to experience as known by an Other" (*The Meaning of God in Human Experience*, 1912, p. 278). W. H. Sheldon (*The Strife of Systems*, 1918) proposes a dialectical reconciliation of idealism and realism which in its method and its ultimate concept (creativity) is more idealistic than realistic.

tellectualistic Kant of the *Critique of Pure Reason*, the voluntaristic and moralistic Kant of the *Critique of Practical Reason*, and the æsthetic and intuitionistic Kant of the *Critique of Judgment*. Reject the conception of the thing-in-itself, as all later Kantians proceed promptly to do, and mind and its creations are left in possession of the field. There then arises a rivalry of emphasis among the several modes of the mind's activity, thought, will, and feeling. Each, after absorbing the other two, may claim to be the original and generative principle of experience and reality.

There was nevertheless a marked difference between the new post-Kantianism and the old. While the original followers of Kant rejected the thing-in-itself, they rejected it as unknowable, rather than as a symbol of metaphysical reality. They found through thought or will or feeling a *knowable* thing-in-itself, and hence abandoned the critical method for speculative metaphysics. In this they were followed as a rule by the British and American idealists whom they influenced. The new German post-Kantians, on the other hand, not only rejected the thing-in-itself, but renounced the metaphysical aspiration which it symbolized. They endeavored to remain faithful to the critical method, as opposed both to "dogmatic" metaphysics, and to that "psychologism" which describes the phenomena of the mental life without recognizing their necessary epistemological implications. They conceived philosophy, in other words, to be the study of the presuppositions of the sciences. Hence it was not so much a question of the relative reality of thought, will, or feeling, as of the

SPIRITUALISM AND IDEALISM

relative priority of the categories of physics, ethics, and æsthetics.

The so-called "Marburg school" arose as an attempt to purify the Kantianism of Lange.[1] It derived its name from the fact that its members, including Lange, were professors at the University of Marburg. Its principal representatives were HERMANN COHEN (1842–1918) and his pupil and associate PAUL NATORP (1854–1924).[2] Their systems were symmetrical and closely similar, and followed the order of the Kantian *Critiques*, of which Cohen was a leading commentator.[3] In developing his own thought Cohen began with a *Logic of Pure Knowledge* and added an *Ethics of Pure Will* and an *Æsthetic of Pure Feeling*.[4] To the first of these corresponds Natorp's *Logical Foundations of the Exact Sciences*, while the latter's ethical teachings are developed in his *Social Pedagogy*.[5] Both writers also paid their respects to religion, and both recognized the need of some unifying conception by which natural science, ethics, and art should be united. Cohen found such a conception in a general "cultural consciousness" (*Kultur-*

---

[1] § 11.
[2] The most eminent living representative of this school is Ernst CASSIRER (*Substanzbegriff und Funktionsbegriff*, 1910; English trans., *Substance and Function*, 1923). Cassirer's thought has departed far from its Kantian origins, and deals generally with the logic of science, with emphasis on its formal and relational structure, and with special reference to recent developments in physics.
[3] In his *Kant's Theorie der Erfahrung*, 1871; *Kant's Begründung der Ethik*, 1877; and *Kant's Begründung der Æsthetik*, 1899.
[4] *Logik der reinen Erkenntnis*, 1902; *Ethik des reinen Willens*, 1904; *Æsthethik des reinen Gefühls*, 1912.
[5] *Die logischen Grundlagen der exakten Wissenschaften*, 1910; *Sozialpädagogik*, 1899.

bewusstsein), while Natorp found it in that "subjectivity" of consciousness which, being transcended in natural science, ethics, and art, has afterward to be restored and taken account of in a general or philosophical psychology.[1]

Kant's thing-in-itself being left out of the account, there was no longer for Cohen any occasion for retaining the distinction between the receptivity of intuition and the spontaneity of the understanding. Thought is no longer an organization of the given, but a purely creative process. To be and to be thought (the act and the product) are one and the same thing.[2] Instead of nature as object (*Gegenstand*) there is only science and its task (*Aufgabe*). And science means for Cohen the exact science which derives its form from mathematics. Hence when he draws up his table of the categories, he places first those which constitute the laws of thought itself (origin, identity, contradiction); then the categories of pure mathematics (reality, multiplicity, allness); then those of applied mathematics (substance, law, concept); and finally those of "modality" (possibility, actuality, necessity).

The most distinctive feature of Cohen's doctrine of the categories is the fundamental place which he assigns to that of "origin" (*Ursprung*). This category signifies the power of thought to construct by a synthesis of un-

---

[1] *Allgemeine Psychologie nach kritischer Methode*, 1912. Natorp also published historical studies of Plato and of Pestalozzi (*Plato's Ideenlehre*, 1903; *Der Idealismus Pestalozzi's*, 1919), which exercised a considerable influence on his own thought, especially his ethics. His *Vorlesungen über praktische Philosophie* was published posthumously in 1925.

[2] *Logik der reinen Erkenntnis*, p. 18.

SPIRITUALISM AND IDEALISM

decomposable elements. Such elements Cohen thought to be provided by the infinitesimal of calculus. The same idea appears among the categories of mathematics as the category of "reality." Mathematics is essentially quantitative or numerical, and assumes an element to be measured or counted. This element by which quantities can be generated, and which is not itself quantitative, but individual and "real," is again the infinitesimal.

As logic formulates the principles of "pure thought," so ethics formulates the principles of "pure will." As the pure or logical thought finds expression in natural science, so pure or moral will finds expression in jurisprudence (*Rechtswissenschaft*). The pure will is that will divested of all particularity and dependence on private inclination, which is presupposed in the moral consciousness. Such a will is found in a system of individual wills governed by law, in which the individual appears only in his universal capacity, as a subject of rights and duties defined by the system as a whole. There is, in other words, no moral will save in the state. Individuals are moral only by virtue of their participation in the organized group, or by virtue of the juristic status which such an organized group confers on them. The moral will of the individual is the universal or corporate will which works in him, and which it is his right and duty to realize.

While in the logic of natural science Natorp differed from Cohen in many points of detail, it is in ethics that the former displayed his own peculiar bent and genius. He found a transition from logic to ethics in the fact that the last word of science is an unfinished task (*Aufgabe*) pointing beyond experience, an *ought*-to-be (*Seinsollen*), over and above the world of being (*Sein*). Ethics is the science of this ideal of reason, which, as essentially shared and objective, is the bond that unites human wills into a community. Like Plato, Natorp thought of individuals as having their true interest and *rationale* in an organized society, and arranged the practical activities and corresponding virtues in three stages: desire and temperance; regulated will (*Willensregelung*) and courage; reason and truth. These moral levels are represented in society by economic, governmental, and creative (cultural) activities. To establish the ascendancy of the creative reason over both industry and politics, and thus to unite individuals into a community of cultural aspiration, is the object of education, and the programme of Natorp's "idealistic socialism."

On the whole it is characteristic of the Marburg school to retain intact the threefold structure of the Kantian critiques. The data of philosophy are the three great systems, natural science, ethics, and art, and the task of philosophy is to bring to light their presuppositions or implicit reason. But there are two suggestions looking toward a further unification. In the first place, although both Cohen and Natorp manifested a rationalistic and even positivistic temper in giving first place in their systems to the logic of natural science, there was (notably in Natorp) a recognition of the fact that even the logical reason is a practical or moral activity, directed to an end. In the second place, both philosophers suggested that there is a mode of consciousness embrac-

SPIRITUALISM AND IDEALISM

ing logic, morality, and art: for Cohen it was the "cultural consciousness," and for Natorp the common and unifying aspect of subjectivity or immediacy. These suggestions point in the direction of the schools of Windelband and Rickert, and of Dilthey and Eucken.

§ 20. Ethical and Cultural Idealism in Germany. Windelband. Rickert. Dilthey. Eucken. Simmel

WILHELM WINDELBAND, who was born in 1848, was the founder of a school which, because of his connection with Freiburg, Strassburg, and finally (until his death in 1915) with Heidelberg, is commonly called the "Southwest German School," or "School of Baden." Although Windelband proceeded in the main directly from Kant, he owed much to Lotze's doctrine of "validity" (*Geltung*).[1] Influenced also by Kuno Fischer,[2] he gave special attention to the history of philosophy, which he treated not as a succession of distinct systems, but as a continuous development of ideas, forming part of the general process of human culture.[3] His own thought was set forth in a series of addresses and articles, and in an *Introduction to Philosophy*, published in 1914.[4]

Starting with the Kantian view of knowledge as consisting in the formative and synthetic act of judgment,

[1] § 14.
[2] (1824–1907). A famous teacher and historian of philosophy.
[3] The most important of his numerous historical writings is the *Geschichte der Philosophie*, 1878–1880; 2d edition, 1892; English trans., *History of Philosophy*, 1893.
[4] *Einleitung in die Philosophie*; 2d edition, 1920; English trans., 1921. The *Präludien*, 1884 (6th edition, 1919), was a compilation of his shorter writings. Cf. also his *Principien der Logik* in vol. I of the *Enzyklopädie der philosophischen Wissenschaften*, 1912.

Windelband contended that there is a deeper reflexive act in which the judgment itself is claimed to be true or false. Over and above "the intellectual element of bringing contents together in a certain relation," there is an act of *assent* or *dissent* on the part of the will,[1] which defines a realm of *validity* (*Geltung*). Truth is not a correspondence of ideas to facts, but a satisfaction of the fundamental demands of the subject. Since, however, it is assumed that truth is *universally* valid, the subject which truth satisfies cannot be the particular empirical subject, but must be a "logical consciousness in general" (*logisches Bewusstsein überhaupt*). The sciences which realize the demands of this subject are both rational (like mathematics) and empirical. Among the empirical sciences there is an important difference between the "natural" and the "historical" sciences (*Naturwissenschaften* and *Geschichtswissenschaften*). Both are synthetic and selective, in accordance with the demands of the subject; but while the former is "nomothetic," seeking generalization, uniformity, and order, and expressing itself in types and laws, the latter is "idiographic," dealing with concrete individuals in so far as these possess some moral, æsthetic, or cultural value.[2]

Over and above logical value, or validity, there are ethical and æsthetic values, which in their universality again imply the claims of a transcendental subject. The moral consciousness, or consciousness of duty, is interpreted as the demand upon the individual of a

---

[1] *Introduction to Philosophy*, pp. 170-171.
[2] *Ibid.*, pp. 201-208.

SPIRITUALISM AND IDEALISM

communal will, which is in turn a manifestation of "the idea of humanity" or "the moral order of the world."[1] This universal life expresses itself historically as successive systems of culture,[2] in whose realization it is the duty of the individual actively to participate. Æsthetic values rise above moral values in their freedom from that sense of need and incompleteness which accompanies desire and will; and express themselves most perfectly in the unself-conscious inspiration of genius.

Religion does not signify a fourth realm of value, but only the supersensuous aspect or reference of logical, ethical, or æsthetic values. Common to all three realms is the implication of a normative consciousness (*Normalbewusstsein*), whose ideals remain in human experience as an unfulfilled aspiration. Religion is the demand for their complete realization in the perfect or "holy," or for the overcoming of that duality between value and reality which is both the impenetrable mystery and the essential characteristic of human life.[3]

Windelband's thought has been further developed by HEINRICH RICKERT, who succeeded him at Heidelberg in 1916.[4] Rickert differs from Windelband in a more

---

[1] *Introduction to Philosophy*, p. 291.
[2] *Präludien*, edition of 1916, vol. II, p. 191.
[3] *Ibid.*, p. 358.
[4] He was born in 1863. His most important writings are *Der Gegenstand der Erkenntnis*, 1892, and *Die Grenzen der naturwissenschaftliche Begriffsbildung*, 1896. Other prominent members of the school were Hugo MÜNSTERBERG (1863–1916), called to America as professor at Harvard University in 1892, and eminent in psychology (*Grundzüge der Psychologie*, 1900) as well as in philosophy (*Philosophie der Werte*, 1908; English trans., *The Eternal Values*, 1909); and Max Weber (1864–1920), whose *Gesammelten Aufsätze zur Religionssoziologie* (1920–1922) and other writings are of importance in the field of the philosophy of the social sciences, especially of economics.

explicit and thoroughgoing reduction of the "is" (*Sein*) to the "ought" (*Sollen*). Being is known to us only as an object of *judgment*, but "the peculiar logical essence of judgment is affirmation and denial, approval or disapproval, or an attitude to a value."[1] In other words, the knowing subject pronounces judgment in obedience to the requirements of an "ought," which it recognizes as *binding* upon it, and therefore as independent of its private inclination. This ideal objectivity transcends all actuality and all subjectivity, not as being unrelated to them, but as being a standard to which they are obliged to conform. Taken in the context of knowledge at least, there is no meaning in the "is," without an ulterior reference to what is valid (*gilt*) or true. "It is valid or true or good that '*a*' should be '*b*,'" underlies the simple "*a* is *b*" of the empirical consciousness. Thus Rickert's philosophy centres in the Kantian "primacy of the practical reason," and has been characterized as "neo-Fichteanism."

Rickert was first concerned to *distinguish* between the "ought" and the "is," or between value and actuality (*Wert* and *Wirklichkeit*), but felt also the need of reconciling them, as two aspects of the same being, or original felt immediacy, which he characterized as "immanent meaning" (*immanent Sinn*).[2] A problem of unification arose also within the realm of values itself. The logical consciousness has its own peculiar duty to perform, and its own peculiar norms or categories. In obedience to these norms the cognitive subject develops

---

[1] *Der Gegenstand der Erkenntnis*, 1904, p. 108.
[2] *System der Philosophie*, 1921, vol. I, pp. 235–255.

two groups of sciences: the natural sciences, which generalize and explain in terms of laws; and the cultural and historical sciences,[1] which deal with concrete individuals and activities. The sciences of culture are thus governed by the norms of the logical subject. But, on the other hand, science is itself a branch of culture, having its historical development. It belongs, along with æsthetics and the mystical experience (*der Mystik*), to the "contemplative" and asocial branch of culture, which is contrasted with the "active" branch; the latter embracing ethics, the pursuit of happiness (*die Erotik*), and religion (the pursuit of perfection). There is thus a rivalry in Rickert between a tendency to subject culture to the demands of the theoretical consciousness, as being the content of a special branch of science; and a tendency to subject science to the demands of a more general consciousness, as being a special branch of culture.

This latter tendency, so pronounced in Windelband and Rickert, to accept *the history of culture* as the ultimate object of philosophy, or to view reality as the progressive unfolding of a universal life, whose norms are embodied with equal authority in science, morality, and art, found its most radical and consistent expression in WILHELM DILTHEY (1833–1912). This philosopher, who succeeded Lotze at Berlin in 1882, distinguished himself as a biographer of Schleiermacher and

---

[1] *Kulturwissenschaften* or *Geschichtswissenschaften*. Rickert rejects the conception of "spiritual sciences" (*Geisteswissenschaften*) because he regards psychology as one of the natural sciences.

Hegel, and as a critic and historian of literature.[1] Owing to his broad cultural interests, he was many-sided both in his sources and in his influence; and his philosophy, being essentially unsystematic, never found any unified expression.[2]

Dilthey's central doctrine was the immediately apprehended "coherence of life" (*Lebenszusammenhang*) which expresses or objectifies itself in a "world-view" (*Weltanschauung*).[3] In his doctrine of an inner revelation or active, personal experience (*Erlebnis*) of life, he approximated the position of spiritualism, as opposed to that of criticism; and in conceiving "life" as embracing cognitive, moral, and æsthetic factors in a single, irrational creative impulse, he approximates the position of romanticism, as distinguished from both the logical emphasis of the Marburg school and the moral emphasis of the school of Baden.

The difference between the natural and spiritual sciences for Dilthey is the difference between objective cognition (*Erkennen*) and the sympathetic insight (*Verstehen*) by which we grasp the inwardness of life.[4] This sympathetic insight extends beyond ourselves, and enables us to realize the unity of the great cultural manifestations of life. Here Dilthey turned, as did Windelband and Rickert, to a philosophy of history. We can-

---

[1] *Leben Schleiermachers*, 1870; *Die Jugendgeschichte Hegels*, 1905; *Die Einbildungskraft des Dichters*, 1887; *Das Erlebnis und die Dichtung*, 1905.

[2] The most important writings for the purpose of understanding Dilthey's fundamental position are the *Einleitung in die Geisteswissenschaften*, 1883; *Der Aufbau der geschichtlichen Welt in den Geisteswissenschaften*, 1910; *Weltanschauung, Philosophie und Religion*, 1911.

[3] *Weltanschauung*, etc., pp. 7, 29.

[4] *Der Aufbau der geschichtlichen Welt*, etc., p. 10.

SPIRITUALISM AND IDEALISM

not deduce the course of history from any set of first principles, but we learn the rich possibilities of life from its progressive unfolding in modes of general outlook or world-view, each of which is relative to special social and natural conditions. Every such world-view is at one and the same time a conception of reality, an order of values, and a governing purpose.[1] Of such world-views Dilthey recognized three general types: *naturalism*, which is materialistic, utilitarian, and deterministic; *idealism* of the *subjective* or active type, in which mind is conceived as free and creative; and *objective idealism*, which expresses itself in a contemplation of the universal harmony. The first is exemplified by Hobbes and Hume; the second by Plato and the post-Kantians; the third by Spinoza and Goethe.

Dilthey's use of the historical and psychological methods, his cultural preoccupations and his insistence on *life* as the central reality and the proper theme of philosophy, have had a widely pervasive influence upon contemporary German thought. His immediate followers have interpreted his "sympathetic insight" (*Verstehen*) in terms of the scale of values which is characteristic of the personal life, and have made a moral-psychological study of mental "types" distinguished by the dominance of some one end over others.[2] Dilthey's philosophy also pointed in the direction of two

[1] *Weltanschauung*, etc., p. 28.
[2] Cf., *e. g.*, E. Spranger, *Lebensformen*, 1922. A similar view of the task and rôle of philosophy as self-expression and as interpretation of life appears in H. v. Keyserling, *Unsterblichkeit*, 1907. Cf. also E. Tröltsch (*Die Bedeutung der Geschichte für die Weltanschauung*, 1917), in whom the influence of Dilthey blends with that of Rickert.

relatively independent developments, an activistic spiritualism, and a historical relativism. The former direction of thought is represented by RUDOLPH EUCKEN, pupil of Trendelenburg,[1] professor of philosophy at Basel and Jena, and a writer of wide popularity, both in Germany and abroad.[2] Eucken is an eloquent partisan of spiritualism and idealism against both the naturalistic philosophy and what he deemed to be the deadening and confusing influences of modern life. Like Dilthey he finds in the history of philosophy the record of a spiritual movement to be interpreted in terms of an immediate revelation of the inwardness of life. But his philosophy, like that of Fichte, which it resembles throughout, is a call to arms rather than a historical survey. Spirit is essentially action and struggle, in which there is resistance to be overcome and a victory to be won. Life is a *deed*, and there is no deed without a duality of agent and object (*Keine Tat ohne Zweiheit*).[3] The world is to be construed in terms of the demands of the fullest and most active personal life. This method of taking as the principle of truth the requirements of the whole of life, rather than of the mere intellect, he calls the "noological" method.[4] The world is in a sense

---

[1] § 14.
[2] Born in 1846. His principal writings are: *Die Einheit des Geisteslebens in Bewusstsein und Tat der Menschheit*, 1888; *Die Lebensanschauungen der grossen Denker*, 1890 (English trans., *The Problem of Human Life*, etc., 1909); *Der Wahrheitsgehalt der Religion*, 1901 (English trans., *The Truth of Religion*, 1901); *Das Wesen der Religion*, 1901; *Grundlinien einer neuen Lebensanschauung*, 1907 (English trans., *Life's Basis and Life's Ideal*, 1912); *Geistige Strömungen der Gegenwart*, 3d editio,n 1904 (English trans., *Main Currents of Modern Thought*, 1912).
[3] *Die Einheit des Geisteslebens*, etc., p. 354 and *passim*.
[4] *Grundlinien*, etc., pp. 119 ff.

what we make it. Although Eucken's philosophy is thus a philosophy of faith and of action, it does not employ these categories in any limiting sense. All knowledge is faith in the sense that it springs from the exigencies of action, but the activity whose urge is thus obeyed is that of a universally immanent spirit.

While Eucken thus represents the bolder metaphysical implications of Dilthey's thought, GEORG SIMMEL (1858–1918) construed in more empirical terms Dilthey's view that philosophies and other cultural manifestations are relative to the special circumstances under which they arise. His interest lay not in metaphysical, nor even in historical, generalizations, but in the detailed study of the way in which ideas and ideals arise in response to specific human needs, and in relation to concrete human situations. Assuming, in common with the whole neo-Kantian school, that the spirit constructs its own world, he recognized no universal *a priori* principles by which this construction is determined and rationalized, but *described* it in psychological and sociological terms. Thus in his famous *Philosophy of Money*[1] he traced the change in the meaning or function of money, from a qualitatively distinct thing, having a value in itself, to a symbol and measure of power. Similarly in his ethics, he claimed no final and valid standard, but devoted himself to a study of the genesis of such typical concepts as "ought," or "egoism" and "altruism," and the particular contexts from which

---

[1] *Philosophie des Geldes*, 1900. Simmel has an important place in the development of modern sociology. Cf. his *Soziologie*, 1908.

they derive their meaning.[1] All categories are for Simmel evolved in a certain setting and possessed of a limited and relative truth, in so far as they fit that setting. This relativity is itself the only possible philosophical generalization. A tendency always to transcend its own achievements, or to pass from a relative truth to an absolute, which in turn becomes relative in the light of an ulterior absolute, is the very essence of life.[2]

Eucken's emphasis on the *deed*, and Simmel's interpretation of truth in terms of a life-process which refuses to be embraced under any fixed system of categories, suggest a transition from idealism of the orthodox Kantian type to the new movement variously known as neo-vitalism, activism, or pragmatism.[3]

§ 21. The New Idealism in Italy. Croce. Gentile

The recent development of idealism in Germany reveals a tendency to interpret thought not in terms of its finished product, or in terms of its ideal implications, but rather in terms of its actual process in human life. This tendency to activism and historicity, freed, so far as possible, from every taint of biologism or utilitarianism, appears in the so-called "new idealism," which is the most conspicuous movement in contemporary Italian thought.

BENEDETTO CROCE may be considered as a descendant of German idealism of the post-Kantian type, and also as an exponent of the Italian national tradition.

---

[1] *Einleitung in der Moralwissenschaft*, 1892–1893.
[2] This characteristic *self-transcendence* of life (*Über-sich-selbst-hinausgehen, Sich-selbst-überwinden*) is developed in the author's *Lebensanschauung*, 1918, and *Philosophie des Lebens*, 1920.
[3] §§ 22–25.

The emphasis on history and universal culture, which was characteristic of German thought in the nineteenth century, had in Italy found a much earlier expression in Vico, the philosopher of the Renaissance whom Croce himself did much to rehabilitate;[1] and was also represented among Croce's early contemporaries by notable men of letters, such as De Sanctis and Carducci.[2] Croce, like Vico, came to philosophy by way of historical and linguistic interests. Born in 1866, in the province of Aquila of a Neapolitan family, he settled in Naples, after his university studies in Rome, and adopted the career of a private scholar. This career has been interrupted only by occasional periods of service in public office, as senator and as minister of public instruction.

Beginning as a student of Neapolitan history, he first widened the range of his erudition and then deepened his reflection upon it. As his philosophy grew out of his brooding upon history, so it culminated in the doctrine that philosophy *is* history. The essence of this paradoxical statement consists in the rejection of the common distinction between history as a series of events, and history as a knowledge of these events. The events of history are actions, which imply knowledge, while the knowledge of these events implies a reenacting, as well as a rejudging, of them. The past is history only in so far as it is being relived in the present, and there is no essential difference between those who live in history and those who make history live. History is thus perpetually made and remade by the

---

[1] Giovanni Battista Vico, 1668?–1744. Cf. Croce's *La Filosofia di Giambattista Vico*, 1911.
[2] Francesco De Sanctis, 1817–1883; Gisué Carducci, 1835–1907.

162 PHILOSOPHY OF THE RECENT PAST

reflective performance of man, who brings to bear such philosophy as he has in him.[1]

Although Croce follows Hegel in his basic idealism and in his view of reality as a spiritual life of which the driving force is a conflict of opposites, he rejects the latter's "panlogism." [2] This modification of Hegel has had two effects. On the one hand, reality is with Croce unambiguously identified with the actual *process* of spirit, rather than with its eternal or "absolute" logical structure; while, on the other hand, Croce recognizes the autonomy of the several non-logical manifestations of spirit such as art and nature. Croce's philosophy is notable for its pluralistic flavor and breadth of inclusiveness. It is unfolded in three main works, the *Æsthetic*, the *Logic*, and the *Philosophy of the Practical*, the last embracing *Economics* and *Ethics*, and the whole setting forth the four fundamental forms of human activity.[3]

Rejecting every sort of transcendence, there will be as many aspects of reality as there are modes of conscious life. The latter is divisible into the theoretic and the practical consciousness, of which the first is again divisible into *intuition* and *intellect*. Intuition is genu-

---

[1] *Logic*, English trans., p. 494. Cf. *Teoria e Storia della Storiographia*, 1920 (English trans., *History, Its Theory and Practice*, 1921).

[2] *Saggio sullo Hegel*, 1913 (English trans., *What Is Living and What Is Dead in the Philosophy of Hegel*, 1915).

[3] The work on History, mentioned above, constitutes the fourth volume of the *Filosofia dello Spirito*. The other volumes appeared as follows: *Estetica come scienza dell' espressione e linguistica generale*, 1902 (English trans., *Æsthetic*, 1909); *Logica come scienza del concetto puro*, 1905 (English trans., *Logic*, 1917); *Filosofia della Pratica: Economica ed Etica*, 1909 (English trans., *The Philosophy of the Practical*, 1913). His writings include, in addition to the above, a large number of essays (many contributed to his review called *La Critica*) and of works in literary and political history.

most ultimate and inclusive sense of the term. The thinker which thus generates the world is not human in the naturalistic or limiting sense. There is a pure and universal spirit, having its own essential and abiding nature, and its inherent order of categories and phases, but manifesting itself and manifesting *only*, in the thinking activity of man.

But while Gentile's thought retains the features broadly characteristic of the "new idealism," he rejects what is pluralistic in Croce. To accept the division of spirit into distinct realms is to belie its essential unity. Spirit must be so conceived as to generate multiplicity out of itself without loss of identity. The key to such a view of spirit is afforded by self-consciousness, in which consciousness makes an object of itself and in so doing changes itself. It is the same spirit which is both subject and object, both creator and created. Consciousness in its subjective aspect is art, in its objective aspect religion, and in its reflective synthesis,—or subject-making-an-object-of-itself,—philosophy. Thus it is philosophy which most perfectly reveals the nature of spirit; and since it is the life of spirit which constitutes the universe, one is led again, although in a somewhat modified sense, to the teaching that history, philosophizing, and reality are all one.[1]

[1] While the new idealism of Croce and Gentile flourishes mainly in Italy, it has exercised no little influence in other countries, notably in England, where it numbers among its followers J. A. Smith ("The Philosophy of Giovanni Gentile," and other articles in the *Proceedings of the Aristotelian Society*, 1914–1920; and *The Nature of Art*, 1924); and H. Wildon Carr (*The Philosophy of Benedetto Croce*, 1917; and *The General Principle of Relativity*, 1920).

PART IV

VITALISM, VOLUNTARISM, AND PRAGMATISM

§ 22. The Will to Power. Nietzsche

Both idealism and spiritualism affirm the priority of mind to physical reality, the former in respect of knowledge, the latter in respect of being. The essential nature of mind being revealed on the plane of human self-consciousness, its categories are accordingly those of thought, moral will, æsthetic feeling, or artistic genius. But it is possible to hold that its essential nature is revealed upon a more primitive plane, in irrational desire, sense-perception, blind will, instinct, or life. These possibilities provide a gradation of views in which spiritualism approximates naturalism. According to a strict spiritualism, the key to reality is to be found in logic, ethics, or æsthetics. According to an intermediate view, widely held in the eighteenth century, this key is to be found in psychology. Progression in this direction leads finally to the view that the key is to be found in biology. This view may be identified with spiritualism, in that it subsumes physics and chemistry under a "higher" science; or it may be identified with naturalism, on the ground that it subsumes logic and ethics under a "lower" science. Or, if we conceive the sciences to form an order from physics through biology to logic, ethics, and æsthetics (the so-called "normative sciences"), we may say that naturalism reduces to physics, and spiritualism to the normative sciences; while the third view reduces both ends to the middle, or conceives

VITALISM AND PRAGMATISM 169

both physics and the normative sciences in terms of biology.

This third view is known as *vitalism*,[1] when the intention is to affirm the irreducibility of life to physico-chemical terms; it is known as *voluntarism* (or *activism*), when the intention is to identify life and will, and so to obtain a biological interpretation of the content of psychology; it is known as *pragmatism* or *instrumentalism*, when the intention is to extend biological categories to the normative sciences, and in particular to logic. An exponent of this general type of philosophy may emphasize one of these aspects, but can scarcely fail to manifest all three.

FRIEDRICH NIETZSCHE represents this general tendency in its cultural and moral applications, and in the manner of the poet and reformer rather than of the systematic philosopher. The individualistic emphasis of this tendency, which is always marked, finds in Nietzsche its most extreme and powerful exponent. He was born in 1844, and the earliest formative influences on his thought were received from the teachings of Schopenhauer, from his personal friendship with the great composer Richard Wagner,[2] and from his studies

---

[1] A movement known as "neo-vitalism" began in Germany with Johannes Reinke (b. 1849; *Die Welt als Tat*, 1899). Its most eminent representative is Hans DRIESCH (b. 1867): *Der Vitalismus als Geschichte und Lehre*, 1905 (English trans., *History and Theory of Vitalism*, 1914); *Philosophie des Organischen*, 1908; *Wirklichkeitslehre*, 1917. Two works published in English, *Science and Philosophy of the Organism*, 1908, and *The Problems of Individuality*, 1914, contain translations from several German originals together with added matter.

[2] 1813–1883. Wagner was influenced by Feuerbach and Hartmann, as well as by Schopenhauer.

of classical antiquity,—this last interest leading to his appointment as professor of philology at Basel in 1869. His first important work, *The Birth of Tragedy*,[1] was an interpretation of history as a conflict between the principles of Dionysus and of Apollo, the first representing the blind but rich and inexhaustible force of life, the latter the balance, repose, and harmony of form. Although Nietzsche saw in history the inevitable and fertilizing conflict of these principles, it was the first which he emphasized, and which he found embodied in the philosophy of Schopenhauer and the music of Wagner. But, while he admired the voluntarism of Schopenhauer and the *Siegfried* of Wagner, he revolted against the former's cult of resignation and the latter's Christianized *Parsifal*. At the same time that he thus diverged from his earlier masters he came under the influence of naturalism both in its positive and in its negative aspects. Positively, he adopted the standpoint of scientific biology; negatively, he accepted the gospel of disillusionment;[2] in both he sought refuge from the too easy and too edifying enthusiasms of romanticism. To this naturalistic stage of his development belong his *Human, All Too Human*, and his *Joyful Wisdom*.[3] Finally, in his *Zarathustra* and later works[4] he found a unity of his own in the philosophy of "the will to

---

[1] *Die Geburt der Tragödie aus dem Geist der Musik*, 1872 (English trans., 1910).

[2] It was this which attracted him to Voltaire.

[3] *Menschliches, Allzumenschliches*, 1878 (English trans., 1909–1911); *Die fröhliche Wissenschaft*, 1882 (English trans., 1910).

[4] *Also sprach Zarathustra*, 1882 (English trans., *Thus Spake Zarathustra*, 1909); *Jenseits von Gut und Böse*, 1886 (English trans., *Beyond Good and Evil*, 1907); *Zur Genealogie der Moral*, 1887 (English trans., *The Genealogy of Morals*, 1910); *Der Wille zur Macht* (incomplete), 1888 (English trans., *The Will to Power*, 1909–1910).

VITALISM AND PRAGMATISM 171

power," which is both the Dionysian principle in culture and the vital principle in nature. Meanwhile his failing health, which was in part a result of work in the ambulance service during the Franco-Prussian War, and which had compelled him to abandon his professorship in 1879, aggravated his extreme sensitiveness and emotional instability. A stroke of paralysis produced, early in 1889, a state of entire mental collapse which lasted until his death in 1900.

In the naturalistic phase of his thought Nietzsche abandoned his earlier leanings toward a spiritualistic metaphysics, and adopted the standpoint of biology. But while in so doing he was greatly influenced by Darwin, he was a Darwinian only in a limited sense.[1] Life is essentially a force of self-assertion ("a living thing seeks above all to *discharge* its strength"), and evolution, or the "ascent of the line of life," [2] is the triumph of strength over weakness. Adaptation, or a passive submission to the environment, is the very opposite of life. The course of evolution is determined by the will: those survive who *will* survive. This is both a description of fact, a practical appeal, and a standard of value. The good life is the life which by the might of its superiority both *can* survive and *deserves* to survive. There is but one obligation upon man, which is to stretch his powers to their limit, and thus to become "super-man." "The Superman is the meaning of the earth. Let your will say: The Superman *shall* be the meaning of the earth." [3]

---
[1] § 6.
[2] *Beyond Good and Evil*, § 13; *Will to Power*, p. 674. Cf. §§ 491–492.
[3] *Thus Spake Zarathustra*, Prologue, § 3.

In terms of this central vitalistic and voluntaristic conception Nietzsche interpreted knowledge, ethics, and religion. He was not interested in proofs, but rather in the psychology, of that which calls itself knowledge. Psychology is "the path to the fundamental problems."[1] Nietzsche's own belief that "the world seen from within" is "Will to Power, and nothing else,"[2] has to be accepted as a sort of initial revelation, confirmed by the fact that once granted it provides an explanation of all other beliefs. Thus the belief in the reality of objects arises from "the sensations of strength, struggle, and resistance."[3] "The greater part of the conscious thinking of a philosopher is secretly influenced by his instincts." Behind all logic there are "physiological demands for the maintenance of a definite mode of life." Man could not live without "logical fictions," errors, falsity, foolishness—the only question being "how far an opinion is life-furthering, life-preserving, species-preserving, perhaps species-rearing." All philosophy is a "confession, a sort of 'involuntary and unconscious autobiography.'"[4] The deeper truth of the disillusioned will to power is revealed only to the initiated, or to a sort of intellectual aristocracy. It would be cheapened and vulgarized by general agreement. It is not attested by its contributions to "happiness and virtue," but rather by its dangerousness, or by the fact that only the strong can endure it.[5] The supreme test of the strong man is his ability to endure the vision of

---

[1] *Beyond Good and Evil*, § 23. [2] *Ibid.*, § 36.
[3] *Will to Power*, vol. II, §§ 533, 552.
[4] *Ibid.*, §§ 3, 4, 6. [5] *Ibid.*, §§ 39, 43.

VITALISM AND PRAGMATISM 173

that "eternal recurrence" which is the fundamental law of nature. He will endure it because his very strength ennobles existence and makes tolerable the thought of its eternity.[1]

Turning to "the genealogy of our moral prejudices," Nietzsche finds that the root of all value is to be found in the superior man's sense of his own nobility.[2] The true ethics, which serves as the norm by which to judge the diversity of moral codes, is this aristocratic ethics of self-affirmation and mastery. Any moral code is to be condemned which does not promote *"the maximum potentiality of the power and splendor* of the human species." Judged by this standard the traditional code of self-denial and commiseration, "the morality of pity," is "the most sinister symptom of our modern European civilization." [3] It is the code of the slavish herd, a code of envy and helplessness, which since it disparages nobility and idealizes weakness is the very inverse of true morality.

Christianity itself is judged and condemned by the same standard. It is not a question of proving or disproving God's existence, but of determining the ennobling or degrading effect of the Christian cult. The Christian God is to be rejected because as conceived by Christianity he is not divine. The "Christian God" is "the poor people's God," "one of the most corrupt concepts of God ever arrived at on earth," because "everything strong, brave, domineering, and proud has been

---

[1] *Thus Spake Zarathustra*, part III, ch. LX.
[2] *Genealogy of Morals*, Preface, § 2, and First Essay, § 2.
[3] *Ibid.*, Preface, §§ 5, 6.

174 PHILOSOPHY OF THE RECENT PAST

eliminated" out of it; it is "God degenerated to the contradiction of life, instead of being its transfiguration and its eternal *yea!*"[1]

§ 23. The Impulse to Life. Bergson

HENRI BERGSON is affiliated with the French spiritualistic movement represented by Ravaisson, Lachelier, and Boutroux, but he is none the less sharply distinguished by his naturalistic leanings. While French spiritualism proclaims the fundamental reality of the creative will, this reality is held to reveal itself most profoundly in its higher flights—in thought, morality, art, and religion.[2] While will as active and free is prior to reason construed as passive necessity, this is only because will is itself essentially rational, in the sense of being governed by its own inherent ends of truth, goodness, beauty, and universality. With Bergson, on the other hand, the essential nature of metaphysical reality is revealed in the natural life and consciousness. Philosophy takes as its point of departure not the standards and ideals of the normative sciences, but the empirical content of biology and psychology. Instead of substituting a soaring intellectual faculty or aspiring

---

[1] *The Antichrist*, §§ 17, 18 (English trans., *The Case of Wagner*, etc., 1896, pp. 257–258).

[2] The most distinguished contemporary exponent of this French tradition is Maurice Blondel (b. 1861; *L'Action*, 1893; *Le Proces de l'Intelligence*, 1922). Blondel affirms the primacy of will. His method, however, is that of rigorous proof (adapted to the circumstance that in the knowledge of the will the knower and the known are one); and he distinguishes over and above the empirical will of biology and psychology a deeper metaphysical will, which is universal, and which expresses itself in the ideals of ethics and religion.

reason for the mundane categories of natural science, Bergson disparages all rational or conceptual thought in behalf of instinct and intuition. Nor is the failure of intellect to grasp reality merely an accidental effect of man's limited experience, as with Bradley, but it is a radical failure. Intellect misrepresents and falsifies reality, and in endeavoring to remedy its own defects it only aggravates them. Its failure is due to the fact that reality does not possess that systematic and logical structure which the intellect represents, but a fluidity, mobility, continuity, and perpetual novelty, which is given only in the immediate and sympathetic sense of life.

Bergson was born in 1859 and was for twenty years (1901-1921) professor at the Collège de France. His brilliancy of style, the cosmopolitan and versatile quality of his genius, and the daring and novelty of his ideas have given him an influence greater than that of any other living philosopher. His three principal works all adopt a psychological or biological point of departure. The *Immediate Data of Consciousness*[1] distinguishes between the fundamental self whose states are inseparably fused and "interpenetrating," and the "spatialized" self of discrete states; ascribing freedom to the former, and determinism to the latter. *Matter and Memory*[2] investigates the relation of mind and body, and affirms that consciousness in the form of "pure memory" is independent of the brain, which is an instrument of action.

[1] *Essai sur les Données immédiates de la Conscience*, 1889 (English trans., *Time and Free Will*, 1910).
[2] *Matière et Mémoire: Essai sur la Relation du Corps avec l'Esprit*, 1896 (English trans., 1911).

176 PHILOSOPHY OF THE RECENT PAST

Finally, *Creative Evolution*[1] traces the course of this same active reality in the physical cosmos, where, assuming the forms of plant and animal life, it opposes and overcomes the resistance of inert matter.

The entire philosophy is pervaded by a fundamental duality which appears in many forms, such as spirit and matter, life and mechanism, time and space, freedom and determinism, interpenetration and juxtaposition, spontaneity and rigidity, intuition and intellect. This duality can best be approached through the last of these oppositions, as being the most radical and distinctive.

Bergson's view of knowledge begins with a distinction between perception and memory in their *purity*—a distinction of kind and not of degree.[2] Pure perception coincides with ever-changing present existence; it participates in the immediately given reality, following its changes, prolonging them in bodily movements, and having an intimation of their infinite spread and continuity. Pure memory, on the other hand, is the whole past preserved in the shape of unconscious psychical states, unlocalized, and irrelevant to the present moment of action.

But perception and memory in their purity are thus distinguished only in order to trace their interaction. That which merges them, or qualifies the one by the

---

[1] *L'Évolution créatrice*, 1907 (English trans., 1911). The most important of his other writings are: *Le Rire*, 1900 (English trans., *Laughter*, 1911); "Introduction à la Métaphysique," in *Revue de Métaphysique et de Morale*, 1903 (English trans., 1912); *L'Energie spirituelle*, 1920 (English trans., *Mind-Energy*, 1920); *Durée et Simultanéité*, 1922.

[2] *Matter and Memory*, English trans., p. 72.

VITALISM AND PRAGMATISM

other, is the body; which is not an organ of representation, or "maker of images," but a "centre of action," employing both perception and memory, and binding the two together for *practical* purposes. Ordinary perception is not, like pure perception, preoccupied with the object, but introduces memory, which evokes from the remoter past "those former perceptions which are analogous to the present perception"; and so suggests "that decision which is the most useful." At the same time, memory focusses or "condenses" the immediate past; and so "by allowing us to grasp in a single intuition multiple moments of duration, it frees us from the movement of the flow of things, that is to say, from the rhythm of necessity."[1]

Similarly, ordinary memory is restricted to those images which are relevant to the present. Pure memory is the whole past indiscriminately preserved, the deep reservoir of spiritual energy which in the interest of present action has to be held below the threshold of waking consciousness, and allowed to manifest itself only in so far as it is appropriate and useful. In dreams, delirium, hallucination, false recognition, insanity, or revery the flood-gates are inadvertently opened, and consciousness, though enriched, loses touch with actualities. Normally this under-mind is drawn upon only so far as it can be brought to bear on the present practical situation, and it is only memory in this limited sense of vigilant and economical recall that is dependent on the body.[2]

[1] *Matter and Memory*, p. 303. Cf. pp. 81 ff.
[2] *Mind-Energy*, English trans., II, IV, V.

Thus ordinary perception is not a theoretic contemplation of reality, but a plan of action. The object is reduced to that which is to be done about it. The very cleavages that divide one object from another are an effect of artificial isolation. The perceived object tends to become little more than a sign of what is to be expected, or an occasion for drawing upon the past as a guide for the future. The corporeal aspects of the world —its static, orderly, spatial, and quantitative characters, are an effect of fixation and abridgment; while its qualitative characters are an effect of "condensation." Science is only the elaboration and refinement of this same tendency, already manifested in perception and in common-sense. The most exact sciences, such as physics, mathematics, and logic, are not, as is commonly supposed, the most theoretical, the most purely cognitive; but, on the contrary, are the most conventional, schematic, and therefore practical. The intellect reaches the acme of artificiality and of utility in conceptual thinking. "To try to fit a concept on an object is simply to ask what we can do with the object, and what it can do with us. To label a certain object with a certain concept is to mark in precise terms the kind of action or attitude the object should suggest to us."[1] The intellectualized object is reality reduced to the utmost passivity, while the intellectualizing of it is reality raised to the highest activity. The activity of the subject and that of the object are thus inversely proportional.

Reality is to be known as it is only by "intuition";

[1] *Introduction to Metaphysics*, English trans., p. 41.

VITALISM AND PRAGMATISM 179

and to obtain this metaphysical insight it is necessary to recognize and discount the bias of our practical needs. "By unmaking that which these needs have made, we may restore to intuition its original purity and so recover contact with the real." As regards our own inner life and freedom, instead of objectifying ourselves and so bringing ourselves under the spatializing, decomposing, and deterministic categories of science, we can, by changing the point of view, become immediately aware of that "duration *wherein we act*" (*durée réele*) and wherein "our states melt into each other." [1] We may obtain a similar immediate knowledge or intuition of material reality by relaxing the tension of practical effort, and restoring the wealth of content which our practical effort has contracted into instantaneous and abbreviated summaries. Then the qualities of perception dissolve into a myriad of little movements, and the minor differences which were negligible for practical purposes emerge again in all their multiplicity. The homogeneous and static space becomes a plenum of movement, a "concrete extension, continuous, diversified, and at the same time organized." [2]

It is evident that the dualism of intellect and intuition is by no means unreconciled. In the first place, while the intellect falsifies reality in the interest of practice, it does so not by fabrication, but by *selection*. Of the lower or purely material aspect of nature it renders an approximately adequate account, and even in the sphere of life and mind it fails through insufficiency or

[1] *Matter and Memory*, English trans., pp. 241, 243–244.
[2] *Ibid.*, pp. 241, 243, 244.

partiality, rather than through any absolute contrariety to fact. Intellect does not create out of whole cloth, but isolates, arrests, and over-simplifies, through dwelling exclusively on something which *is* there, but which is only a small *fragment* of what is there. Furthermore, it has to be recognized that this very falsification is achieved in the interest of practice. Intellect is an indispensable adjunct of life where, as in man, this reaches the highest degree of emancipation from matter. When thought is construed as a plan of action, science becomes an infinite multiplication of the possibilities of action, which, through its very extension of the range of determination in the object, increases the indeterminateness or freedom of the agent.

As Bergson's cognitive dualism is reconciled through conceiving intellect in terms of selection and the requirements of action, so his metaphysical dualism is reconciled through conceiving life and matter as only the inverse and complementary aspects of the same process, the one being its "making" and the other its "unmaking." Reality is movement or activity which has different degrees of intensity, and two opposite tendencies.[1] Positively it tends to be gathered all at once into a moment of creation, or focussed to a point of pure activity; negatively it tends to relax and dissolve, and thus to become more repetitive, homogeneous, and stagnant.[2]

The course of natural evolution with its upward ten-

[1] Or can the opposition be reduced to the difference of intensity, so that matter becomes a sort of tide-rip marking the projection of the more sluggish upon the livelier current?
[2] Cf. *Introduction to Metaphysics*, English trans., pp. 62–64.

dency and its essential sameness amidst diversity of forms, can be understood only as one original vital impulse (*élan vital*), which has to overcome resistance, and divides itself to conquer. Life is everywhere endeavoring to maintain and increase itself amidst the drag and inertia of materiality. When it succumbs it lapses into mechanism, as in the case of habit. Its first victory is the accumulation and storage of energies which can be explosively released. This is the achievement of plant life. Profiting by this achievement, animal or mobile life diverges in two directions, culminating in the "instinct" of the arthropods and the "intelligence" of the vertebrates. Instinct is capacity to deal directly and infallibly with the object, an adaptation of the organism itself to its immediate environment. Intelligence is a capacity to deal indirectly and experimentally with the object by the fabrication and use of mechanical tools, which are external both to the organism and to the object on which it acts. Instinct enters sympathetically into the inner nature of the object, or goes to the heart of it by penetrating insight, but its variability and its range are narrow. Intelligence remains outside the object, but through the very externality of its methods it is enabled to extend its action widely, and to construct its own world by a limitless conjoining of one mechanism with another. Instinct tends to be unconscious through the fact that its knowledge is a perfect adaptation, translated instantly into action: its knowledge consists in a capacity to *do* the right thing in the given circumstances. Intellect, on the other hand, has more projects than it can fulfil; and it is just this multiplication of possibilities which makes human life so highly conscious and so unpredictable.

The value of life lies in its intensity and activity; and here again the duality of life and matter is softened by the reflection that effort would be impossible without matter. "By the resistance matter offers and by the docility with which we endow it, it is at one and the same time obstacle, instrument, and stimulus." [1] Matter also divides spirit, and individuates it, thus setting the task of the achievement and growth of personality. But Bergson, unlike Nietzsche, never loses sight of the *unity* of life. There appears to have been "some original and essential aspiration of life which could find full satisfaction only in society." "It is the moral man who is a creator in the highest degree—the man whose action, itself intense, is also capable of intensifying the action of other men, and, itself generous, can kindle fires on the hearths of generosity." [2] Bergson's religious imagination is fired by the same idea. With this doctrine of life as a single immense wave spreading outward from the same centre, "we feel ourselves no longer isolated in humanity, humanity no longer seems isolated in the nature that it dominates. . . . All the living hold together, and all yield together to the same push." God is this central radiation of life. "God thus defined, has nothing of the already made: He is unceasing life, action, freedom." [3]

---

[1] *Mind-Energy*, English trans., p. 29.
[2] *Ibid.*, pp. 32–34.
[3] *Creative Evolution*, English trans., pp. 265–266, 270–271, 248.

§ 24. Catholic Modernism. Le Roy

There are two general movements which are associated with the influence of Bergson and with allied tendencies in French thought, philosophical *syndicalism*, and Catholic *modernism*. The former advocates social revolution as an expression and cult of the heroic will.[1] The latter attempts a reconciliation of the Catholic faith with modern science and biblical criticism, through a pragmatic, voluntaristic, or activistic interpretation of religious truth. The underlying philosophy of modernism appears in the thought of ÉDOUARD LE ROY,[2] who succeeded Bergson at the Collège de France, and combined the latter's philosophy with that of Poincaré. Extending Poincaré's idea of the conventionality of scientific theories[3] to science as a whole, both in its logical and in its empirical aspects, he finds that things, laws, and concepts, all alike, exist only by definition. The

---

[1] The most prominent representative of this movement is Georges Sorel (1847–1922). Cf. his *Réflexions sur la Violence*, 1909 (English trans., 1912).

[2] Le Roy was born in 1870. His most important writings are: "Science et Philosophie," *Revue de Métaphysique et de Morale*, vol. VII, 1899; "Le problème de Dieu," *ibid.*, vol. XV, 1907; *Dogme et Critique*, 1907.

A prior and not less eminent philosophical protagonist of modernism is M. Blondel (§ 23). Among its influential leaders were: Antonio Fogazzaro (1842–1911; *Il Santo*, 1905; English trans., *The Saint*, 1906); Friedrich von Hügel (1852–1925; *Catholic Mysticism*, 1914); George Tyrrell (1861–1909; *Christianity at the Cross-Roads*, 1910); Romolo Murri (1870–   , the leader of the Christian Democratic movement in Italy, and author of *La Croce e la Spada*, 1915); and Alfred Loisy (1857–   , the most powerful champion of the cause, and author of numerous works in biblical history and criticism, and of modernist tracts; cf. his *L'Évangile et l'Église*, 1902, and the autobiographical work trans. into English as *My Struggle with the Vatican*, 1924).

[3] § 11.

work of the intellect, even the carving of facts out of the continuum of the given, is to be construed as a self-expression of life. What this life is in its depths is known by intuition, and, above all, in the religious experience. The dogmas of Christianity are to be construed not as theorems, intellectually demonstrable, but as rules of action. Thus "God is a person" means "treat God as a person." Only when dogmas are so conceived is it possible to understand how they should be imposed by authority, and how they should obtain meaning in terms of the religious life.

Modernism was anathematized and, as a Catholic movement, effectually suppressed by the famous Encyclical *Pascendi dominici gregis*, issued by Pope Pius X in 1907.[1] While this document is polemical and harsh in tone, it brings clearly to light the issue between modernism and the traditional philosophy of Catholicism. Modernism attempted to reconcile devoted adherence to the Church as an historic institution and community of worship with entire freedom of scientific research and opinion, and with the spirit of progressivism. This reconciliation was to be effected by an emphasis upon the *religious experience,* as constituting both the heart of religion and the evidence of its truth. The modernists were[2] distinctively Catholic, rather than Protestant, in the spirit of their piety—in their mystical sense of corporate solidarity and union with the past, and in their faith in the transforming power of love. They

---

[1] English versions of this Encyclical may be found in G. Tyrrell, *The Programme of Modernism*, 1908; and P. Sabatier, *Modernism*, 1908.

[2] One speaks of living modernists in the past tense because they are now either excommunicated, silenced, or "indexed."

were men of eminent Christian spirituality. On the other hand, however, they allied themselves unqualifiedly with modern methods in all fields of inquiry. In order to reconcile these two positions they adopted a theory of knowledge entirely at variance with the Catholic intellectual tradition. They were obliged so to conceive the truths of faith as to render them consistent with any results to which free investigation might lead, in church history, biblical criticism, or cosmology. The truths of faith, they taught, are such as can be apprehended *only* by faith, being an expression of the inner needs of the soul, and verified by their quickening effect upon the will. Their value lies not in their reproduction of facts, but in their power to enhance the religious life. The words and concepts in which they are formulated are not descriptions, but symbols, and they must from time to time be reworded and reconceived if they are to preserve their power over the hearts of men. Truths of this sort cannot contradict the findings of science, because they belong to another sphere; nor, on the other hand, can they be disparaged by science, since science itself is also the expression of other and less central needs.

It is not surprising that the writer of the Encyclical should have accused modernists of "subjectivism" and "agnosticism," since they denied the power of the intellect to lay hold on the reality beyond phenomena; of substituting the immediate intuitions of an "interior sense" for the proofs of natural theology and for authentic revelation; of substituting "fideism" for rationalism; of converting the realities of Christian belief into fictions, symbols, and instruments; of making all religious truth relative and transitory, and all religions equally true; of saving religion from science by making it unscientific. Judged by the "Catholic principles" embodied in the scholastic philosophy, modernism is thus a "synthesis of all the heresies," being in direct opposition to the claim that Christian belief rests upon a foundation of objective knowledge firmly and incontrovertibly established by reason.[1]

§ 25. Pragmatism and the Will to Believe. James. Peirce. Dewey. Schiller. Vaihinger

The difference between Bergson and WILLIAM JAMES is the difference between a psychological biology and a biological psychology. Both oppose materialism and mechanism in that they find the centre of reality in the field of life and mind, and both oppose spiritualism of the traditional type in that they interpret life and mind in terms of their observed or felt existence, rather than in terms of their standards or "norms." Both might be described by such phrases as "naturalistic spiritualism" or "spiritualistic naturalism." Both, furthermore, tend to reduce life and mind to common terms. The difference is that while for Bergson these common terms retain a stronger flavor of life, for James they retain a stronger flavor of mind. For Bergson's reality the most adequate term is "activity"; for James's, "experience."

This difference arises, on the part of James, from the

[1] The Encyclical *Pascendi* both suppressed modernism and prescribed scholasticism: "We will and strictly ordain that scholastic philosophy be made the basis of the sacred sciences." P. Sabatier, *op. cit.*, p. 325. Cf. below, § 27.

VITALISM AND PRAGMATISM

influence of the British empirical school, in which he takes his place in the line of succession after Hume and Mill; and from his lifelong preoccupation with psychology. This latter bent sprang both from the psychological emphasis of British empiricism and from his own early training in the biological sciences. Born in 1842, and originally a student of anatomy, chemistry, and medicine, his scientific interest was deepened by his contact with Louis Agassiz.[1] In experimental and physiological psychology he found a fruitful contact between the scientific method and the larger human problems. Through his wide reading and culture, and owing to a profound antipathy to what he took to be the dogmatic negations of science, his philosophical interests took root early in his career and never ceased to dominate him; but it was through his contributions to psychology that they found their first important expression. *The Principles of Psychology*, his greatest work, and of epoch-making importance in the history of this science, appeared in 1890. The volume of essays entitled *The Will to Believe*, published in 1897, brought more clearly to light the broad philosophical implications of his psychology. His theory of truth was published under the title of *Pragmatism* in 1907, and gave its name to the school of which he was now the accepted leader. *The Varieties of Religious Experience* (1902) and *A Pluralistic Universe* (1909) contained his speculations in the field of religion and metaphysics.[2]

---
[1] § 5.
[2] Among the more important of his other philosophical writings are: *The Meaning of Truth*, 1909; and the posthumous publications, *Some Problems of Philosophy*, 1911, and *Essays in Radical Empiricism*, 1912.

From 1880 until 1907, three years before his death in 1910, James was a teacher of psychology and philosophy at Harvard University. His numerous contacts with European scholars, his cosmopolitan outlook and cast of mind, and his extreme versatility combined to spread his influence more widely than that of any other American thinker of his day.

James's psychology contains, over and above a wealth of empirical detail, two central ideas that governed his later philosophical thought. Although disposed to construe consciousness, after the manner of the British tradition, as a manifold of distinguishable states traceable to sense-experience, he insisted upon its *activity* and *unity*. The activity of consciousness is selective, interested, teleological. It attends to this or that within a "theatre of simultaneous possibilities," and thus "carves out" its own world from "the jointless continuity of space and moving clouds of swarming atoms."[1] Especially is this true of the higher faculties of will and intellect, of which the former, by dwelling upon one idea to the exclusion of others, causes it to fill the mind and thus to express itself in outward action; while the latter isolates and integrates "things," imputes reality to them in so far as they are related "to our emotional and active life," and conceives them under whatever aspect may prove most significant and fruitful.[2] The unity of consciousness consists in its through and through connectedness. It is a flowing stream, of which the "substantive" parts shade into

---

[1] *Principles of Psychology*, vol. I, pp. 288–289.
[2] *Op. cit.*, vol. II, p. 295; ch. XIX, XXI, XXII, XXVI.

VITALISM AND PRAGMATISM

one another through the "transitive" parts, and in which every object is surrounded by a "fringe," or accompanied by a "feeling of tendency" through which it passes over into another.[1]

James's theory of knowledge was developed from this psychological standpoint, and is throughout dominated by its two main characteristics: its emphasis on the categories of interest and practice; and its reduction of relations, substances, activities, and other alleged transcendent elements to the continuities of sense-experience. The former motive in James's thought led to his voluntarism and pragmatism, the latter to his "radical empiricism."

James attributed his pragmatic theory of knowledge and its name to CHARLES S. PEIRCE,[2] an American scholar of great erudition and originality, who distinguished himself in physics as well as in philosophy, and was one of the founders of "symbolic logic." According to Peirce, conceptions are to be interpreted in *experimental* terms. The conception of any given object consists of the effects to be anticipated of the object, and

[1] *Op. cit.*, vol. I, ch. IX.
[2] 1839–1914. Peirce did not accept James's theory of truth, but held that truth consists essentially in the agreement of experts—insisting, as scientist and logician, upon the importance of technic. Other striking features of his thought, which influenced Royce as well as James, were his theory of the evolution of natural laws, his theory of the objective reality of chance, and his theory of "signs." The cosmos assumed for him the aspect of the gradual development of a rational order out of chaos. Some of his scattered writings were published in 1923, under the title of *Chance, Love, and Logic*. The article to which James referred as the original source of pragmatism was entitled "How to Make Our Ideas Clear," and appeared in *Popular Science Monthly* in 1878. James's reference to Peirce is in *Pragmatism*, p. 46. Cf. also "What Pragmatism Is?" *Monist*, vol. XV, 1905. For a bibliography of Peirce's numerous papers, cf. *Jour. of Philos.*, vol. XIII, 1916, pp. 733 ff.

these effects, in turn, are to be construed as sensible effects; that is, effects which would have to be taken account of in practice. The conception is thus a general plan of action, or system of expectations, with reference to an object.

James takes this view as his point of departure, and develops what he believes to be its implications. There are two sorts of knowledge—knowledge *by acquaintance* and knowledge *about*. In the former the object is immediately presented, in the latter it is known mediately, or by means of ideas. The function of the idea in knowledge is not to reproduce the object, but to prepare for or lead the way to it. Pragmatism consists, in the first place, in the "method" which interprets our idea of an object as "what conceivable effects of a practical kind the object may involve—what sensations we are to expect from it, and what reactions we must prepare."[1] In other words, the meaning of an idea looks forward to consequences, rather than, as with the traditional empiricism, backward to its sensory original. The truth of an idea will therefore consist in the ulterior satisfaction which it affords, either through the fulfilment of the sensory expectation or the success of the reaction. But since we form expectations only for the purposes of action, their fulfilment is only an incident of practical success, and we may say of truth as a whole that it consists in the utility or "working" of ideas; or that "the true . . . is only the expedient in our way of thinking."[2] The value of having expectations fulfilled lies in its enabling us to *deal* with the existing sit-

[1] *Pragmatism*, pp. 46–47. [2] *Ibid.*, p. 222.

VITALISM AND PRAGMATISM

uation; so that the final justification of all ideas, like their meaning, is to be found, not in their logical structure or in their origin, but in the service which they render to the will. It is the will which accounts for our having ideas at all, and it is the will to which in the last analysis they are accountable.

This being the case, moral or æsthetic demands may properly be decisive where ideas are not verifiable in the limited sense of the fulfilment of sensory expectations. This is James's famous doctrine of the "will to believe," in which, following Renouvier, he argues against the scruples of positivists such as Clifford.[1] Since science itself arises in response to practical demands, it cannot overrule such demands. It is impossible to avoid extra-empirical beliefs, for the very omission of them is equivalent to their negation. He who from scientific scruples declines to believe in God is in effect *dis*-believing in God; and sense-experience does not support the negation any more than it supports the affirmation. Since one cannot remain non-committal—since, in other words, there is a "forced option," "our passional nature not only lawfully may, but must decide."[2]

James's doctrine of "radical empiricism" is closely related to the "phenomenism" of Renouvier. It means not only that reality in order to be "debatable" at all shall be definable in terms drawn from experience," but that experience is coherent and self-sufficient *in its own terms*. It does not mean that knowledge is to be limited to the boundaries of actual experience, but that it shall

[1] § 4.   [2] *Will to Believe*, p. 11.

not employ any categories save those that are exemplified in experience. There is no need of invoking any non-empirical type of unity, such as a transcendent substance, or a pure activity, or an *a priori* synthetic consciousness, since experience contains its own bonds, in the shape of "conjunctive relations," which "are just as much matters of direct particular experience, neither more so nor less so, than the things themselves."[1] The most remarkable application of this thesis is to consciousness itself, which is not an entity outside its own experience, but only one type of conjunctive relation *among* these experiences. The same identical terms of "pure experience" taken in one (the causal or energetic) type of relationship constitute "the system of external realities," while taken in another type of relationship they constitute "the stream of our internal thinking."[2]

James's metaphysics, like his theory of knowledge, has both its empirical and its practical mode of approach. Empirically we must take reality to be just what it seems to be, as it is given to us in direct acquaintance: "that distributed and strung-along and flowing sort of reality which we finite beings swim in."[3] Its most characteristic features are those which the ordinary logic rejects. "How can what is manifold be one? how can things get out of themselves? how be their own others? how be both distinct and connected? how can they act on one another? how be for others and yet for themselves? how be absent and present

---

[1] *Meaning of Truth*, pp. xii, xiii.
[2] *Essays in Radical Empiricism*, p. 22. Cf. Mach, § 11.
[3] *Pluralistic Universe*, p. 213.

VITALISM AND PRAGMATISM 193

at once?"[1] Such logical difficulties are, however, created by that very intellectualism which is baffled by them. For intellect deals with things by abstraction and then proceeds as though there were nothing to the thing but what is abstracted. The solution lies not in making more abstractions, but in a return to the original concreteness, where these artificial difficulties do not occur.

It was in this appeal from the self-limiting and self-defeating processes of the intellect to the illumination of intuitive immediacy that James found himself confirmed by Bergson.[2] It enabled him not only to adhere to the empirical standpoint in metaphysics, or to identify reality with experience, but also to accept as a probable hypothesis Fechner's doctrine of a superhuman consciousness, compounded of the experiences of human and infra-human minds.[3] This hypothesis acquires plausibility from the "abnormal or super-normal phenomena" of multiple personality, automatic writing, and mediumship; but above all from the *religious experience*, with its conviction "that we inhabit an invisible spiritual environment from which help comes, our soul being mysteriously one with a larger soul whose instruments we are."[4] The mystical intuition would then be "only very sudden and great extensions of the ordinary 'field of consciousness,'"—"an immense spreading of the margin of the field."[5]

---

[1] *Pluralistic Universe*, p. 260.   [2] *Ibid.*, Lect. VI.   [3] § 14.
[4] *Ibid.*, pp. 298–299, 308–309. Cf. *Varieties of Religious Experience*, Lect. XX.
[5] *Collected Essays and Reviews*, 1920, p. 500.

In this sense a metaphysics which is pluralistic and yet religious obtains a certain "direct empirical verification."[1] But this same view is supported also by the demands of the moral and emotional life. Theism is "the most practically rational solution it is possible to conceive." For there is "not an energy of our active nature of which it does not normally and naturally release the springs. At a single stroke it changes the dead, blank *it* of the world into a living *thou*, with whom the whole man may have dealings."[2] Only the supposition of a finite God of limited responsibility, and an undetermined world, in which what ought to be is genuinely possible, can make the existence of evil tolerable to the moral will.[3] Only the sense of being under God a "faithful fighter" in the cause of righteousness, together with faith in an ultimate victory to which one will oneself have furnished a genuine contribution, can make "life worth living."[4] Thus the pragmatic theory of knowledge and the empirical-pluralistic metaphysics converge in a militant moralism and theistic faith.

After James the most distinguished American representative of the vitalistic, voluntaristic, pragmatic school is JOHN DEWEY.[5] His philosophy is commonly

---

[1] *Pluralistic Universe*, p. 308.   [2] *Will to Believe*, p. 127.
[3] *Ibid.*, essay on "The Dilemma of Determinism."
[4] *Ibid.*, essay on "Is Life Worth Living?"
[5] Born 1859. Cf. his *Studies in Logical Theory*, 1903; *Essays on Experimental Logic*, 1916; *Democracy and Education*, 1916; *Experience and Nature*, 1925. For Dewey's relation to Darwinism, cf. his *Influence of Darwin on Philosophy*, 1910; and above, § 6. Among American philosophers who are classed as Dewey's collaborators or followers are: James H. Tufts (*Ethics*, 1908); George H. Mead ("Definition of the Psychical,"

Thomist doctrines, second, such amendment of them as might be required by the advances of science, and, third, their reformulation in terms calculated to convince a modern mind.

The first part of this programme has led to a profound study, employing modern methods of historical scholarship, not only of Thomism but of the whole scholastic epoch.[1] The other two parts of the programme have led to the study of modern science and philosophy, a restatement and extension of Thomist principles, and their adaptation to the method and problems of contemporary philosophical inquiry. There have been three prominent centres of interest in systematic neo-Thomism: the Seminary of St. Sulpice in Paris,[2] the Institute of Philosophy, founded in 1871 as a branch of the University of Louvain, and achieving instant fame through the work of DESIRÉ MERCIER;[3] and the Jesuit College of Stonyhurst in England.[4]

[1] This historical branch of the movement is represented by the work of Cl. Baeumker and M. Grabmann in Germany, M. de Wulf in Belgium, and É. Gilson in France.

[2] Represented, for example, by Albert Farges, whose Études philosophiques (1886–1907) offers a Thomist-Aristotelian interpretation of modern physics, mathematics, biology, physiology, and psychology.

[3] 1851–1926; author of many standard works, both historical and systematic. Cf. his Sommaire du Cours de Philosophie selon Saint Thomas d'Aquin, 1884–1890 (English trans., Manual of Modern Scholastic Philosophy, 1900). On becoming Cardinal he was succeeded at Louvain by M. de Wulf, whose Introduction à la Philosophie neo-scolastique was published in 1904 (English trans., 1907).

[4] The most prominent representatives of this school are: Thomas Harper (1852–1893; Metaphysics of the Schools, 1879–1884); Joseph Rickaby (Moral Philosophy, 1889); Leslie J. Walker (Theories of Knowledge, 1910). The best-known American writers of the neo-scholastic school are Brother Azarias (1847–1893; Essays Philosophical, 1896); and William Turner (History of Philosophy, 1903).

A more recent school, rapidly attaining prominence, is that of Milan, represented by A. Gemelli and F. Olgiati, and by the Rivista di filosofia neo-scolastica. This school attempts a compromise with idealism.

The "golden wisdom of St. Thomas," freed of its excessive emphasis on syllogistic logic, its Ptolemaic astronomy and astrology, its doctrine of angels, and other unscientific or antiquated features, comprises the following doctrines: the reality of universals *in re*, that is, as the ideal essences of existent substances; the interpretation of motion as the tendency of a thing to realize (actualize) its nature; the conception of substance as that which exists by itself; the distinction between "matter" and "form" as aspects of substances, ordinarily inseparable; the conception of the soul as activity, undecomposable and therefore immortal; the proofs of God as first and final cause of nature; a libertarian ethics, in which man is conceived to attain happiness by a realization of his essentially rational nature in the love of God as truth; and, finally, an intellectualistic and realistic epistemology.

It is the scholastic theory of knowledge, with its metaphysical implications, which determines its orientation among the schools of recent and contemporary philosophy. Neo-scholasticism affirms that metaphysical opinion is inescapable, and that metaphysical knowledge is possible; hence its rejection of the sceptical, agnostic, and positivistic forms of naturalism. Metaphysical knowledge is possible through reasoned inferences from the facts of experience—hence the rejection of empiricism. The doctrine that the truth is one, universal and changing, whether it be truth of reason, or the truth of revelation, leads the neo-scholastic to repudiate (as relativistic) every species of pragmatism, even when invoked in support of Christian dogma.[1] Finally, the

[1] *Cf.* "Modernism," above, § 24.

neo-scholastic wages relentless war upon Kantianism, and upon all the varieties of idealistic metaphysics which have emanated from this source. To put a Kantian construction upon knowledge would mean that God and his thought of the world were one, whereas God is distinct from the world, which is his free creation. A Kantian interpretation of knowledge would imply, furthermore, that the human mind in knowing the truth is united with the mind of God; whereas man, like nature, is a creation—in the image of God, but as a separate substance. Idealism leads to pantheism, and the only theory of knowledge consistent with theism is an epistemological dualism, in which the objects of knowledge, *qua* real, are "not affected by the fact of (their) becoming known"; and in which the idea in the creative mind of God "reproduces itself in our mind through the instrumentality of the objects in which it is embodied."[1] In other words, there is inherent in the nature of the intellect a capacity to escape subjectivity, and to refer beyond the mind both to the real objects of nature and to their ulterior Cause.

§ 28. Realism in Germany. Meinong. Husserl

The most important of recent realistic movements in Germany[2] is that which was influenced by the psychol-

---

[1] L. J. Walker, *op. cit.*, pp. 48, 687.
[2] Realism of a different type is represented by O. Külpe (1862–1915), who developed experimental psychology in the direction of the study of the "thought-process." Külpe's realism consists essentially in an insistence on the *transcendence* of the object of knowledge. In relation to history and to other selves, knowledge must transcend both actual and possible experience, so that we have not explained and justified knowledge until we have accounted for the affirmation of a reality which is revealed through both sense and thought, but which lies beyond both. This problem Külpe undertook to solve in his unfinished work,

ogist Franz Brentano,[1] who derived from his studies of Aristotle and scholasticism a view of mind as "intentional." It is characteristic of psychical activity, according to this thinker, to be directed primarily upon *objects*, which may either exist or not exist; and only secondarily, in retrospect, upon itself. Alexius Meinong,[2] student of Brentano at Vienna in 1874, and after 1882 professor at the University of Graz, developed a branch of philosophical investigation which he called "theory of objects" (*Gegenstandstheorie*), which differs from psychology and theory of knowledge in abstracting from the relation to the empirical subject, and from metaphysics in transcending the realm of existence. "Object" in this generalized sense includes not only

Die Realisierung (1912–1920). His *Einleitung in die Philosophie*, 1895, has been translated into English (*Introduction to Philosophy*, 1897). Cf. also his *Philosophie der Gegenwart in Deutschland*, 1911 (English trans., *The Philosophy of the Present in Germany*, 1913). Other realists are: H. Volkelt (*Erfahrung und Denken*, 1886; *Gewissheit und Wahrheit*, 1918); and E. Becher (*Naturphilosophie*, 1914).

Standing somewhat apart from the main currents of recent philosophy is Harald Höffding (1843–   ), the eminent Danish thinker. He terms his philosophy a "critical monism," meaning that while unity is the goal of thought, this goal is never attained, owing to the stubborn multiplicity and perpetual novelty of things. Höffding's view may be termed "realistic" in that thought is only a part of reality, which enables us to adapt ourselves to reality, but which cannot be proved to be typical of it. Höffding's most famous work is his *Religionsphilosophie* (1901; English trans., 1906), in which he defines religion as the belief in the *conservation of values*. Cf. also his *Ethik*, 1888; *Philosophische Probleme*, 1902 (English trans., with a Preface by W. James, 1905); *Der Menschliche Gedanke*, 1910. In all of his doctrines Höffding was profoundly influenced by Sören Kierkegaard (1813–1855), the most important Scandinavian philosopher of the nineteenth century.

[1] 1838–1917. *Psychologie vom empirischen Standpunkte*, 1874.

[2] 1853–1920. Among his more important writings are the following: *Psychologisch-ethische Untersuchungen zur Wert-Theorie*, 1894; *Über Annahmen*, 1902, 1910; "Über Gegenstandstheorie" in *Untersuchungen zur Gegenstandstheorie und Psychologie*, 1904; *Über emotionale Präsentation*, 1917; *Zur Grundlegung der allgemeinen Werttheorie*, 1923.

THE REVIVAL OF REALISM

that which exists, like a physical thing, and that which merely "subsists" (*Bestehen*), such as qualities, numbers, or propositions; but even that which, like the "round square," can neither exist nor subsist, although it can be referred to and thought about.

It is peculiarly characteristic of Meinong to distinguish between judging (with conviction) and merely considering or "assuming" (*Annehmen*); and to insist that even this latter act, tentative and non-committal as it is, nevertheless addresses itself to a peculiar kind of complex object, which can be verbally expressed only by a clause beginning with the conjunction "that." Thus "a white horse" is an object (*Objekt*) in the narrower sense of that which may be perceived, or of which I may form an idea; while "*that* the horse is white" is an "objective," which can be an object (in the broader sense of *Gegenstand*) only when one judges or assumes "that" such is the case. Objects stand to one another, furthermore, in a relation of "superior" to "inferior," or of higher to lower order, the former being "founded" upon or presupposing the latter, as "the difference between red and green" presupposes "red" and "green." Although the object of a mental act is "immanent," in the sense of being within range of, or *before*, the mind, it has to be distinguished from the content (*Inhalt*), which is *in* the mind. This latter is always existent, present and psychical, like the mental act itself; while the object may be non-existent, past or future, or physical.

Meinong has also been largely influential in securing recognition for a new branch of philosophy known as "theory of value,"[1] which deals with the general principles applicable to all the senses in which things can be good or bad. His own peculiar doctrines appear in his view that value appertains only to "objectives"; or is the content of feeling when this is mediated by judgments or assumptions. The measure of the value of an object is the pleasure and pain felt on the assumption of its existence or non-existence. This particular kind of objective, or what one feels *should* exist, he calls a "dignitative"; just as he terms what one desires *to* exist, a "desiderative." Values have, in other words, that peculiar *non-existent objectivity* which is so basic a feature of Meinong's whole philosophy.

EDMUND HUSSERL,[2] like Meinong, was influenced by Brentano, and, like Meinong, he has formulated a new branch of philosophical investigation, which he calls "phenomenology" (*Phänomenologie*). This is a descriptive study of consciousness, or (since it is essentially characteristic of consciousness to have objects), a study of consciousness-of-objects. It is distinguished from ordinary science, including psychology, by its attitude (*Einstellung*). This peculiar phenomenological attitude is contrasted with the primary or "natural" conscious act, which is directed upon the object and takes it to

[1] Cf. also Ch. von Ehrenfels, *System der Werttheorie*, 1897. The most prominent American representative of this tendency, modified by the influence of Windelband and Rickert (§ 19), is W. M. Urban, *Valuation*, 1909.

[2] Born 1859. His principal work is his *Logische Untersuchungen*, originally published in 1900–1901. His later views have appeared in revisions of this work (1913–1921) and in his *Ideen zu einer reinen Phänomenologie und phänomenologischen Philosophie*, 1914. He is professor at the University of Freiburg.

THE REVIVAL OF REALISM

be real. By reflection the naïve, dogmatic attitude may be "reduced," or devitalized. One now no longer *lives* in the perceiving act, or views the object *through* it, nor does one (as in psychology) study the act in its natural environment; but one takes a detached position from which the object appears as simply the objective aspect of the act. It is like the difference between *believing* in God and thinking of myself as believing in God. In the latter case the belief is not asserted, but simply noted —God becoming only the objective component of the act. Phenomenology is thus purely descriptive in method; is capable of perfect certainty, because it makes no claims beyond what is immanent in consciousness; and has universality because as dealing with the nature of objective reference in general it holds of all objective experiences in particular, whether theoretical or practical, and so underlies all the sciences and arts.

Assuming the phenomenological attitude, what do we find? First of all, that consciousness consists of acts directed to objects. But this is only a small part of the story. It is characteristic of Husserl's genius to multiply and refine distinctions rather than to reduce them to systematic unity. Consciousness may be viewed as lying between two poles, the ego and the object. On the side of the ego lies the subjective attitude with its various qualitative forms, such as believing, doubting, considering, or willing; and its modes of apprehension, such as presentation, representation, or symbolism. On the side of the object lies the object itself, and its "sense" (*Sinn*) or ideal character. Midway between the two lies the datum or content, such as images or sensory experience. This may all be briefly stated as an analysis of the structure of meaning, in which it appears: (1) that there must be *some one* (the "I") who means it, and who takes (2) a particular kind of meaningful *attitude* (theoretical or practical); (3) he must have something to mean *with* (a datum), which embodies his meaning, and (4) he must take this, or mean with it, in a certain *way* (as a sign or revelation of the object); (5) he must mean *something*, or there must be something meant (the sense of his meaning), and (6) he must mean this *of* something (the object).

Whether this view is to be deemed realistic or idealistic is largely a matter of emphasis. The analysis of the cognitive process contains many realistic suggestions. The relation of the subject to the object is essentially one of seeing and intending, and implies that the object is approached or addressed, rather than constituted, by knowledge. Thus the physical object cannot be presented except in partial aspects or in perspective, so that there is a large element of uncertainty and error in perception; but what *is* presented is a part of the object, and the residual parts are such as may in turn be presented. Universals, on the other hand, can be wholly given, in a sort of intellectual vision or intuition of essences (*Wesenserschauung*). Similarly, the certainty of phenomenology lies in the fact that it does not "intend" any more than is given. Here even the perceptual object may be absolutely known, because it is "reduced" to what is immanent in the act of perception. All these considerations suggest that objects are both independent of consciousness and capable of being more or less adequately brought within it.

On the other hand, Husserl's growing tendency to identify phenomenology and metaphysics is suggestive of idealism. For the subject-matter of phenomenology is consciousness. In phenomenology all objects of consciousness assume the character of being objects-of-consciousness. From this point of view we are compelled to say not that the relation of the object to consciousness is that of being intended or seen—a relation in which the object is prior, and into which it may enter without prejudice to its independence; but that it is of the very nature of objects that they *should* be intended or seen, or that the complex operation of conscious objectification creates reality in the act of knowing it.

§ 29. Realism in England and America. Russell. Moore. Alexander. Santayana. Whitehead

BERTRAND RUSSELL[1] forms the connecting link between Meinong and the realism which emerged on English soil as a reaction against the sceptical outcome of empiricism in Hume, and of intellectualism in Bradley. Russell believes that philosophy can be rescued from this predicament, and at the same time reconciled with science, only by the adoption of a reformed logic. His treatment of logic resembles Meinong's "theory of objects" (*Gegenstandstheorie*) in that it provides for a realm of entities which are neither physical nor psychi-

[1] Born 1872, and for some years fellow of Trinity College, Cambridge University. His most important philosophical works are: *Critical Exposition of the Philosophy of Leibniz*, 1900; *Principles of Mathematics*, 1903; *Principia Mathematica* (with A. N. Whitehead), 1910–1913; *Our Knowledge of the External World*, 1914; *Analysis of Mind*, 1921.

cal existences—neither things nor thoughts—but which may be referred to, meant, and described. The subject-matter of mathematics belongs to this realm, and one of Russell's most signal contributions to contemporary thought is his unification of logic and mathematics; logic borrowing from mathematics its symbolic method, and mathematics borrowing from logic its fundamental premises.[1]

Russell describes his philosophy as a "logical atomism," in order to indicate his acceptance of the fundamental multiplicity of things, as revealed in analysis. He does not mean that the world is composed of corporeal atoms which are physically divisible from one another, but of relations, facts, and particular items which are *distinguishable* from one another without losing their meaning. Logic itself is atomistic in that it deals with propositions,[2] which are essentially *relational* in structure and hence analyzable into simpler components. As between any two expressions of the same logical form the corresponding parts are interchangeable. Thus in the proposition "John is mortal," "James" may be substituted for "John" without altering the meaning of the remainder of the proposition.

[1] Mathematics and logic thus merge into one branch of knowledge, which may be called (according to differences of emphasis) "mathematical" or "symbolic logic," or "the philosophy of mathematics." The most important contributions to this branch of knowledge (in addition to those of Russell and his collaborator, A. N. Whitehead) have been made by G. Boole (1815–1864), G. Frege (b. 1848), G. Peano (b. 1858), L. Couturat (1868–1914), E. Schroeder (1841–1902), and C. S. Peirce (§ 25).

[2] Or, more precisely, "propositional functions," that is, expressions containing variables and convertible into propositions by assigning values to the variables. Thus "x is mortal" is a propositional function, while "John is mortal" is a proposition.

THE REVIVAL OF REALISM

This Russell argues against the view that a proposition is an indivisible unity such that if any of it is changed, all of it is changed.

The confusions and contradictions of thought (including the so-called "paradoxes" and "antinomies") which have brought discredit on the intellect can all be avoided by a more scrupulous logic, which recognizes its essentially relational character, and observes the requirements of logical form. Most of the traditional difficulties are due to talking nonsense, that is, to combining words in ways which grammar permits but which logic forbids. Modern mathematics, escaping by the use of symbols the confusions arising from language, has already cleared up the most important of the traditional intellectualistic difficulties, those, namely, connected with infinity and continuity.

The intellect, being thus purified, is capable of providing the necessary support to sense-experience. Pure empiricism has failed because it has been unable to provide nature with order and structure. Attempts have been made to remedy this defect by invoking unobservable entities behind experience, or the miraculous intervention of a synthetic mind. The difficulty is escaped if one construes the factual world as constituted of *systems* of *particulars:* the particulars being sensed, the systematic relations logically conceived or judged. A fact is known by "description," when it is known only by its systematic relations as judged; it is known by acquaintance, or in perception, when to this knowledge of its logical structure there is added the sensible presence of its constituent particulars.

Following James, Russell construes the particular existences of sense as ground common to the physical and the psychical realms. The sense-datum is either physical or psychical, according to the causal relations in which it is viewed. Hence the physical world, or the world of science, is composed of the same stuff as our sensory consciousness. Matter and "things," and all the entities of physical science (such as electrons), are only highly complex systems or "constructions" of the same experiential data which in other types of systematic unity make up minds. The physical object is the system of what are commonly called its appearances, while a mind is a system of "perspectives," made up of all the appearances from a certain locus when that locus is occupied by a brain. Psychology is concerned with the particular appearances in their detachment from the object to which they belong, in their dependence on the brain, and in the peculiar kind of causation that governs them. The causation characteristic of minds Russell refers to as "mnemic causation."[1] It consists in the function of *meaning* as dependent on past experience, habit, and association.

Russell's ethics is divisible into two parts, his examination of the traditional problems of moral philosophy, and his social creed. The former leads him to an acceptance of "intrinsic" good and evil, as fundamental and irreducible notions, which are bound up with no concrete subject-matter, such as pleasure and pain, and are independent of existence or non-existence. Moral

---

[1] *Analysis of Mind*, ch. IV. The idea is attributed by Russell to R. Semon (1859–1918), *Die Mneme*, 1904 (English trans., 1921).

THE REVIVAL OF REALISM 215

values, such as "right" and "wrong" attach to actions which either produce or are judged to produce the best results.[1] Russell's social creed is individualistic, pacifistic, and pessimistic as regards the existing political and economic system.[2] His general outlook on life is one of disillusionment rather than of faith. The acceptance of the teachings of science undermines the common religious beliefs, and throws the emancipated mind upon its own resources. Renunciation of vulgar hopes paves the way to a worshipful contemplation of beauty, a proud acceptance of fate, and a courageous loyalty to one's vision of the best.[3]

Through all of the numerous representatives of the realistic tendency in England and in America there runs this same doctrine that knowledge (whether sense-perception or thought) addresses itself to reality, and at some point embraces it, but without compromising its independence. G. E. MOORE [4] presses the distinction between the object (such as the sense-quality) *of* which one is aware, and the *act* of awareness; insisting that it is essentially characteristic of such an act of awareness that "its object, when we are aware of it, is precisely

---

[1] "The Elements of Ethics," in *Philosophical Essays*, 1910.
[2] *Proposed Roads to Freedom*, 1919.
[3] "The Free Man's Worship," in *Philosophical Essays*, 1910.
[4] A highly analytical and critical thinker, born in 1873, and professor of mental philosophy in the University of Cambridge. Cf. his "Refutation of Idealism," published together with other essays in his *Philosophical Studies*, 1922. The writer who stands closest to Moore, in method as well as in doctrine, is C. D. Broad (*Perception, Physics, and Reality*, 1914; *Scientific Thought*, 1923; *The Mind and Its Place in Nature*, 1925). Cf. also J. Laird, *Problems of the Self*, 1917; and *A Study in Realism*, 1920.

what it would be, if we were not aware."[1] S. ALEXANDER[2] construes knowledge as an act of contemplation whose object is "compresent," the act itself being experienced immediately or "enjoyed." American realists fall, for the most part, into one or the other of two groups, known as "neo-realists" and "critical realists."[3] The former group has argued for the immediate presence both of physical existence in perception and of logical (or mathematical) subsistence in thought. The latter group, represented most conspicuously by G. SANTAYANA,[4] has distinguished between the general natures or "essences" which are immediately given, and the transcendent "existences" to which these are referred. According to this view, all that one can directly

---

[1] *Op. cit.*, p. 29.

[2] Born in 1859, and until recently professor of philosophy in the University of Manchester. A long interval separates Alexander's earlier work on the ethics of evolution (*Moral Order and Progress*, 1889) from his recent realism. He is notable among the exponents of realism for his constructive, metaphysical interest. Cf. his *Space, Time and Deity*, 1920.

[3] Each of these schools has published a co-operative volume, the former *The New Realism* (1912), by E. B. Holt, W. T. Marvin, W. P. Montague, R. B. Perry, W. B. Pitkin, and E. G. Spaulding; the latter *Essays in Critical Realism* (1920) by D. Drake, A. O. Lovejoy, J. B. Pratt, A. K. Rogers, G. Santayana, R. W. Sellars, and C. A. Strong.

The more important systematic works of these writers are: Holt, *Concept of Consciousness*, 1914; Montague, *The Ways of Knowing*, 1925; Perry, *General Theory of Value*, 1926; Spaulding, *The New Rationalism*, 1918; Drake, *Mind and Its Place in Nature*, 1925; Pratt, *The Religious Consciousness*, 1921, and *Matter and Spirit*, 1922; Sellars, *Critical Realism*, 1916, and *Evolutionary Naturalism*, 1922; Strong, *Why the Mind Has a Body*, 1903, and *A Theory of Knowledge*, 1923. For Santayana, cf. below. ¦An allied view, combining realism and pragmatism, and metaphysical in its emphasis, is to be found in J. E. Boodin's *A Realistic Universe*, 1916.

[4] Born in Madrid in 1863 of Spanish parentage, long resident in America as professor of philosophy in Harvard University, and at present living in Europe. Cf. his *Life of Reason*, 1905; and *Scepticism and Animal Faith*, 1923.

THE REVIVAL OF REALISM

grasp in intuition is *what* the object is, if there is such an object; while *whether* there is such an object or not can only be taken on "faith," or pragmatically. Both of these groups affirm that there is knowledge of an extramental reality, and that at least the *character* of this reality is envisaged in our conscious experience.

While all contemporary realists agree that in cognition the mind somehow apprehends reality rather than constitutes it, there are wide differences of opinion as to the nature of mind. At least three views are distinguishable. Moore, like Meinong and Husserl, is disposed to construe mind in terms of acts having a unique and irreducible character of intentional awareness. Others[1] are disposed to agree with James in construing mind as a peculiar type of *relationship* (such as "meaning") whose terms are the same as those which, when otherwise related, compose the physical world. A third group, including Alexander and the American neo-realists, conceive mind in terms of the activities of an organism endowed with a nervous system, while calling attention to the fact that these activities lie upon a different plane from that which is ordinarily dealt with in physiology and biology.[2]

Realism is disposed to a metaphysical "pluralism"[3] through emphasis on the category of relation, whether

[1] Cf. F. J. E. Woodbridge, "Nature of Consciousness," *Jour. of Philos.*, vol. II, 1905.

[2] This view is closely related to the contemporary psychological movement known as "behaviorism," according to which the *mind is* what, in its higher and more complex developments, the *body does*. Russell's view may be said to be a combination of this view with the "relational" view.

[3] Realists like Meinong, and Husserl in his earlier stages of development, represent a tendency in realism to avoid metaphysics, in a manner analogous to the "critical" method in idealism.

of the empirical or logical variety. Materialism and spiritualism tend to a monism of substance; idealism, to a monism of the cognitive act, or to the embracing of all reality within a single knowing mind. But through the realistic conception of relations, the differences of the world may compose an orderly structure without becoming inseparably one. Otherwise, realism is divided, in respect of metaphysics, between a tendency to "neutralism" and a tendency to naturalism. By the former is meant the view that reality cannot properly be characterized either in physical or in mental terms, but only in more primitive terms which underlie this distinction. Thus sense-qualities and relations, for example, are regarded as intrinsically neither physical nor mental, but as possessing a character common to these two realms. The naturalistic tendency, on the other hand, arises from the view that while, as regards their composition as revealed in analysis, physical and mental reality are both secondary, the order and history of existence are determined by physical laws, so that mind can be said to be a product of physical nature. This does not, however,[1] mean that mind is a product of ponderable matter, or of "merely" mechanical causes; for physical nature, as reinterpreted in terms of the content of perception and thought, assumes a character which reduces its difference from mind to one of degree rather than of kind. Alexander and others[2] maintain that an *emergence* of purposiveness

---

[1] Except in the case of Santayana, who inclines to a materialistic view of existence and a mechanical view of causation.

[2] Cf. Lloyd Morgan (§ 13) and L. T. Hobhouse, *Development and Purpose*, 1923.

in life and mind is entirely consistent with a physico-chemical view of the lower levels of nature; while Alexander, Russell, and A. N. WHITEHEAD,[1] influenced by the current theory of relativity, conceive physical nature in terms of "events" occurring in "space-time," and thus relieve it of that aspect of inertness in which it once appeared as the very antithesis of mind.

As regards their practical philosophy, there is no agreement among contemporary realists, although their disagreements illuminate their realistic premises. Somewhat similar to Meinong's view of value as an "objective," is Santayana's view that value attaches to "essences" rather than to either physical or psychical existences. Values are immediably objective, but to mistake them for existences is to suffer illusion: to enjoy them one must intuit them without imputing existence to them. Moore, on the other hand, regards value ("intrinsic goodness") as an indefinable quality, which attaches to existent objects in the same sense as the color "yellow"; while Alexander and the American neo-realists incline to the view that value is a psychological character, which the object acquires only by relation to the liking or aversion of a sentient subject.

The most complete metaphysical system thus far produced by Anglo-American realism is to be found in the *Space, Time and Deity* of Alexander. With the ex-

---

[1] Born 1861; sometime professor of applied mathematics at the Imperial College of Science, London, and since 1924 professor of philosophy in Harvard University. His principal philosophical works are: *An Inquiry concerning the Principles of Natural Knowledge*, 1919; *The Concept of Nature*, 1920; *Science and the Modern World*, 1925.

ception of Whitehead,[1] Alexander alone has formulated a definite and original theology. Deity, according to this writer, is to be defined in terms of the principle of emergence, according to which nature rises to successively higher and superimposed levels. Although the human mind is thus far pre-eminent, the principle of emergence implies higher levels beyond, which will be related to the human mind as this in turn is related to the body. Deity is this prospective superiority viewed from below, and God is the supreme eminence or infinite deity, viewed with reverent expectancy by man.

Most contemporary realists are "realistic" in the practical and popular sense, that is, they reject the view commonly held by idealists, that the fulfilment of human aspirations is a universal condition of existence. This idealistic thesis is based on the assumption that reality of every type arises from an act of mind, and is supported by the argument that since mind is essentially purposive or directed to the good, reality as the creation of mind will necessarily be an embodiment of perfection. Realism denies both the assumption and the argument. The nature of the world is judged by facts rather than by ideals. But though the world is not *necessarily* good, neither is it necessarily evil or indifferent to good. The degree of its goodness is a question of experience, or of faith translated into endeavor.

[1] Whitehead's conception of God is briefly stated in his *Science and the Modern World*, ch. XI.

CONCLUSION

§ 30. Tendencies of the Immediate Present

At the opening of the present century realism was sufficiently extended and developed to justify its being ranked among the major currents of modern philosophy. A survey of contemporary European and American philosophy thus reveals four strands: naturalism, both materialistic and positivistic; idealism and spiritualism; pragmatism, voluntarism, and vitalism; and realism. Though these strands are interwoven and interpenetrating, they can nevertheless be unmistakably distinguished as having each a characteristic color of its own.

There are evident signs that these distinctions, although useful for the purpose of the delineation of the philosophy of the recent past, may soon be outgrown. It is possible that philosophy is now nearing the close of a great phase that began with Descartes, and that what it has been customary to term "modern" as distinguished from "mediæval" and "ancient" philosophy, will soon cease to be modern. The philosophy of the present is difficult to characterize for the very reason that the traditional vocabulary begins to be antiquated, while no new vocabulary has as yet come into general vogue. How shall one characterize the fading out of certain distinctions in terms which were designed to accentuate these very distinctions? "Naturalism," "idealism," "pragmatism," and "realism," together with many of the subordinate terms of each of these major philosophical parties, already suggest the battle-cries of a war that is over, and that has ended in a "peace without victory."

Naturalism has ceased to wage war upon religion, and idealism has thus lost its rôle as the protector of the faith. All philosophies have acquired so great a respect for science, both for its method and for the reality of the physical world which it depicts, that there is no longer any occasion for a militant naturalism that shall provide science with a philosophical defense. Similarly, idealism has so far repudiated its subjectivistic origins that the realist, in insisting upon the independent real, has difficulty in finding any one to disagree with him. At the same time, the pragmatist's contention that mind exercises choice, or that thought is governed by purposes and related to the needs of life, is accepted by idealists and realists alike, and proclaimed by all schools of scientific thought.

Perhaps it would be fair to say that there is to-day in all quarters a declining disposition to insist on the exclusive truth of any doctrine, or to argue its negative implications. This may be ascribed in part to the growing interest in common problems, and in part to an increased faith in the possibility of somehow conserving and reconciling the great insights. Along with this spirit of co-operation and conciliation, there is a tendency to reject externality and transcendence, and to think in terms of what is called "experience." It may be that the vogue of this term means nothing more than the belief that philosophy rightly begins with

CONCLUSION

data, and that data must be generally acceptable and capable of affording both a common point of departure and a common court of appeal. In any case, it is a notable fact that idealism in all its manifestations, whether the neo-Hegelianism, neo-Fichteanism, and neo-Romanticism of Italy and Germany, the neo-Kantianism of Germany and France, or the personal idealism of England and America, has less to say about the Absolute and more to say about the observable processes of nature, life, society, and history; so much so, that idealists can now scarcely deny their kinship even with the empiricists and pragmatists whom they once despised. Not less notable is the tendency in naturalistic circles to conceive the physical world, not as a reality behind the scenes which is known only by inference from its phenomenal appearances, but as a system of these appearances; which now cease to be "appearances" in the old sense, and become themselves the very substance and tissue of nature. Similarly, realism is no longer the affirmation of a thing-in-itself, adopted as a refuge from the supposed subjectivity of what is immediately known, but has become the doctrine that the immediately known is itself a genuine aspect of the independent reality.

Whether this philosophical spirit of the times marks the beginning of an era of eclecticism, or an intellectual war-weariness following the polemics of the nineteenth century, or the lull before a new storm of constructive speculation, no man can at this hour confidently predict.

SELECTED BIBLIOGRAPHY

GENERAL WORKS ON THE HISTORY OF RECENT PHILOSOPHY

(* Recommended for Beginners)

ALIOTTA, A.: *Idealistic Reaction against Science*, 1914. Comprehensive critical review of recent tendencies and authors.

ALIOTTA, A.: *Il nuovo realismo in Inghilterra e in America*, 1915.

BOSANQUET, B.: *The Meeting of Extremes in Contemporary Philosophy*, 1921. On relations of neo-realism and neo-idealism.

GUNN, J. A.: *Modern French Philosophy*, 1922.

HÖFFDING, H.: *History of Modern Philosophy* (English trans.), 1908, vol. II. European philosophy from Kant to 1880.

*HÖFFDING, H.: *Modern Philosophers*, 1915. Bradley, Eucken, Boutroux, Mach, Nietzsche, James.

HOERNLÉ, R. F. A.: *Studies in Contemporary Metaphysics*, 1920. Criticisms of naturalism and realism.

HOUTIN, A.: *Histoire du Modernisme Catholique*, 1913.

*JOAD, A. E. M.: *Introduction to Modern Philosophy*, 1924. Russell, James, Bergson, Croce, Gentile.

KRÉMER, R.: *Le Néo-réalisme américain*, 1920.

*KÜLPE, O.: *Philosophy of the Present in Germany*, 1913. Mach, Haeckel, Nietzsche, Fechner, Lotze, von Hartmann, Wundt.

MERZ, J. T.: *History of European Thought in the Nineteenth Century*, 1903. Best available account of the history of science for the period covered.

MOOG, W.: *Die deutsche Philosophie des 20. Jahrhunderts*, 1922.

*MÜLLER-FREIENFELS, R.: *Die Philosophie des 20. Jahrhunderts in ihren Hauptströmungen*, 1923. Present tendencies in Germany.

MUIRHEAD, J. H.: *Contemporary British Philosophy. Personal Statements.* First Series, 1924. Second Series, 1926. Bosanquet, Broad, Hobhouse, Laird, Mackenzie, McTaggart, Lloyd Morgan, Muirhead, Russell, Schiller, Ward, Hicks, Hoernlé, Moore, Smith, Taylor, Thomson.

PARODI, D.: *La Philosophie contemporaine en France*, 1920. French philosophy from 1860 to the present.

PERRIER, J. L.: *The Revival of Scholastic Philosophy in the Nineteenth Century*, 1909.

*PERRY, R. B.: *Present Conflicts of Ideals*, 1918. Present tendencies in their moral, political, and social applications.

PERRY, R. B.: *Present Philosophical Tendencies*, 1912. Critical review of naturalism, idealism, pragmatism, and realism.

PICCOLI, R.: *Benedetto Croce*, 1922. Recent Italian philosophy.

*RILEY, J. W.: *American Thought*, 1923. Royce, Dewey, James, realism.

ROGERS, A. K.: *English and American Philosophy since 1800*, 1923.

RUGGIERO, G. DE: *Modern Philosophy*, 1921. German, French, Anglo-American, and Italian philosophy since 1860, selected and estimated from the standpoint of the Italian idealistic school.

SANTAYANA, G.: *Egotism in German Philosophy.* Nietzsche and other German tendencies.

*SANTAYANA, G.: *Winds of Doctrine*, 1913. Bergson, Russell, American philosophy.

SCHJELDERUP, H. K.: *Hauptlinien der Entwicklung der Philosophie von Mitte des 19. Jahrhunderts bis zur Gegenwart*, 1920. European and American philosophy from 1860 through James.

SCHMIDT, R., Editor: *Die Philosophie der Gegenwart in Selbstdarstellungen.* Five vols., 1922-1924. Becher, Driesch, Meinong, Natorp, Rehmke, Volkelt, Cornelius, Troeltsch, Vaihinger, Croce, Höffding, Ostwald, Keyserling.

SINCLAIR, E.: *The New Idealism*, 1922. Critical summaries of Alexander and other British and American realists.

STEBBING, L. S.: *Pragmatism and French Voluntarism*, 1914. Renouvier, Ravaisson, Boutroux, Bergson.

WAHL, J.: *The Pluralist Philosophies of England and America*, 1925. Bradley, Royce, Fechner, Lotze, Renouvier, James, Russell, American realists.

WHITEHEAD, A. N.: *Science and the Modern World*, 1925. Philosophical significance of recent developments in science.

INDEX

Abbott, C. G., 77
Agassiz, J. L. R., 16, 187
Alexander, S., 216, 217, 219, 220
Ampère, A. M., 10, 11
Apollo, 170
Aquinas, T., 9, 200, 201-204
Ardigò, R., 8
Aristotle, 7, 26, 27, 82, 200, 206
Avenarius, R., 63, 65
Azarias, Brother, 203

Baeumker, C., 203
Bain, A., 13
Bauer, B., 3
Becher, E., 206
Bentham, J., 53, 57, 58
Bergson, H., 113, 174-182, 186, 193
Berkeley, 65
Bernard, C., 11, 108
Berthelot, P. E. M., 11
Blondel, M., 174, 183
Bonald, L. G. A. de, 11
Boodin, J. E., 216
Boole, G., 212
Bosanquet, B., 135
Bossuet, 201
Boutraux, E., 109-111
Bowne, B. P., 144, 145
Bradley, F. H., 15, 130-135, 137
Brentano, F., 206
Broad, C. D., 215
Brockmeyer, H. C., 18
Brunschvicg, L., 125
Büchner, L., 6, 31, 38, 42
Buckle, H. J., 12
Buffon, Count de, *see* G. L. Leclerc

Cabanis, P. J., 97, 100, 101
Caird, E., 130
Caird, J., 130
Calkins, M. W., 145
Carducci, G., 161
Carlyle, T., 15, 17, 54
Carr, H. W., 167

Cassirer, E., 147
Clifford, W. K., 13, 191
Cohen, Hermann, 147-151
Colding, 6
Coleridge, S. T., 15, 17, 54
Collard R., 11, 105
Comte, A., 8, 10, 12, 13, 16, 30, 43-52, 54, 72
Condillac, E. T., 97, 104
Cornelius, H., 63
Cournot, A. A., 12, 45
Cousin, V., 11, 12, 18, 103-107, 202
Couturat, L., 212
Creighton, J. E., 145
Croce, B., 160-166
Cumberland, R., 53
Cuvier, G., 10, 16, 26
Czolbe, H., 6

Dana, J. D., 17
Darwin, C., 6, 10, 14, 16, 17, 20-29, 171
Darwin, E., 20
Darwin, F., 26
Davidson, T., 143
Davy, H., 13
De Sanctis, F., 161
Descartes, R., 77, 78, 80, 101, 104, 110
Deussen, P., 94
Dewey, J., 27, 194, 195
Dilthey, W., 155-159
Dionysus, 170, 171
Drake, D., 216
Draper, J. W., 16
Driesch, H., 169
Dubois Reymond, E., 39
Duhem, P., 67
Dühring, E., 4
Durkheim, E., 44, 71-75

Ehrenfels, C. von, 208
Emerson, R. W., 17
Espinas, A., 72
Eucken, R., 158, 159, 160
Euclid, 69, 70

227

228 INDEX

Faraday, M., 13
Farges, A., 203
Fechner, G. T., 7, 43, 61, 82–86, 193
Ferrari, G., 8
Feuerbach, L., 3, 4
Fichte, I., 7, 81, 92, 99, 154, 158
Fischer, K. P., 7, 151
Fiske, J., 17
Fogazzaro, A., 183
Fouillée, A., 113
Fourier, C., 9
Franchi, A., 8
Frauenstädt, J., 94
Frege, G., 212

Galileo, G., 5
Gallupi, P., 8
Gemelli, A., 203
Gentile, G., 166, 167
Germain, S., 45
Gibbs, J. W., 16
Gilson, E., 203
Gioberti, V., 8
Gobineau, J. A., comte de, 72
Grabmann, M., 203
Gray, A., 17
Green, T. H., 15, 57, 126–129, 130, 131
Grose, T. H., 126
Guyau, J. M., 113

Haeckel, E., 6, 31, 38–43, 44
Hall, G. S., 83
Hamelin, O., 120
Hamilton, W., 15, 31, 32, 54, 59
Harper, T., 203
Harris, W. T., 18
Harrison, F., 45
Hartmann, E. von, 94–96
Hegel, G. W. F., 3, 4, 6, 9, 18, 81, 94–96, 121, 130, 137, 162, 165
Helmholz, H. L. F. von, 5, 83
Henry, J., 16
Herder, J. G., 21
Herschel, J. F. W., 53
Hertz, H., 63
Hobhouse, L. T., 218
Hocking, W. E., 145
Höffding, H., 206
Hoernlé, R. F. A., 135
Holt, E. B., 216
Howison, G. H., 18, 137, 141–143
Hügel, F. von, 183

Hume, D., 15, 32, 53, 65, 97, 105, 110, 115, 122, 126, 127
Husserl, E., 208–211, 217
Hutton, J., 14
Huxley, T. H., 14, 28

James, W., 57, 83, 186–194, 206, 214, 217
Janet, P., 11
Joule, J. P., 5, 13
Jouffroy, T. S., 11

Kant, I., 1, 4–7, 12, 15, 17, 18, 34, 51, 61–63, 81, 98, 99, 105, 111, 114, 115, 116–119, 122, 126–128, 142, 145–148, 151, 154, 160, 200, 205
Kelvin, Lord, 13
Keyserling, H. von, 157
Kierkegaard, S., 206
Kirchhoff, G., 63
Külpe, O., 205

Lachelier, J., 121–125
Ladd, G. T., 83
Laird, J., 215
Lamarck, J. B. de, 10, 20, 21, 24
Lange, A., 4, 44, 60–64
Laplace, P. S. de, 10
Lavoisier, A. L., 5
Le Bon, G., 72
Leclere, G. L., 21
Le Conte, J., 17, 137
Leibniz, G. W. von, 1, 7, 82
Leo XIII, 202
Le Roy, E., 70, 183
Lévy-Bruhl, L., 72, 73, 74
Lewes, G. H., 13
Liebmann, O., 4
Linnæus, C., 26
Littré, M. P. E., 10, 45
Lobatchewsky, N. I., 69
Locke, J., 16, 32, 104
Loisy, A., 183
Lotze, R. H., 12, 62, 83, 85–94, 145, 151
Lovejoy, A. O., 216
Lyell, C., 14, 30

Mach, E., 27, 42, 44, 64–67
Mackenzie, J. S., 135
Maine de Biran, 11, 100–103, 106, 108

INDEX

Maistre, J. de, 11
Malthus, T. R., 23
Mamiani, T., 8
Mansel, H. L., 15, 31, 59
Marvin, W. T., 216
Marx, K., 3, 29
Maxwell, J. C., 13, 63
Mayer, J. R., 5
McCosh, J., 17
McTaggart, J. M. E., 143
Mead, G. H., 194
Meinong, A., 206–208, 211, 217
Mercier, D., 203
Meyerson, E., 125
Mezes, S. E., 137
Milhaud, G., 67
Mill, James, 13, 53
Mill, J. S., 13, 16, 44, 45, 47, 52–59, 65
Milton, J., 26
Mohr, 6
Moleschott, J., 6, 38
Monet, J. B. P. de, *see* Lamarck
Montague, W. P., 216
Moore, A. W., 195
Moore, G. E., 215, 217, 219
Morgan, C. L., 80, 218
Muirhead, J. H., 135
Münsterberg, H., 153
Murri, R., 183

Natorp, P., 147–151
Newton, I., 5, 19, 69
Nietzsche, F., 28, 94, 113, 169–174, 182

Olgiati, F., 203
Ostwald, W., 42
Owen, R., 9

Pasteur, L., 11
Peano, G., 212
Pearson, K., 28, 63
Peirce, C. S., 189, 212
Perry, R. B., 216
Petzoldt, J., 63
Pitkin, W. B., 216
Plato, 8, 27, 150
Poincaré, H., 44, 67–71, 183
Porter, N., 17
Pratt, J. B., 216
Pringle-Pattison, A. S., 143
Proudhon, P. J., 9

Ravaisson-Mollien, F., 12, 106–112
Reid, 11, 32, 105, 106
Reinke, J., 169
Renan, E., 10, 45
Renouvier, C., 12, 113–121, 191
Ricardo, D., 54
Rickaby, J., 202, 203
Rickert, H., 153–155
Riemann, G. R. B., 69
Ritschl, A., 62, 93, 145
Rogers, A. K., 216
Romanes, G. J., 14
Rosmini-Serbati, A., 8, 202
Rousseau, J. J., 99, 100
Rouvroy, C. H. de, *see* Saint-Simon
Royce, J., 18, 136–141, 145, 189
Ruge, A., 3
Russell, B., 77, 80, 211–215, 217

Sabatier, P., 184, 186
Saint-Simon, 9, 45
Sanseverino, C., 9, 202
Santayana, G., 216, 218, 219
Schelling, F. W. von, 7, 11, 82, 99, 103, 106
Schiller, F. C. S., 195
Schlegel, F., 99, 202
Schleiermacher, F. D., 81
Schmidt, C., 3
Schopenhauer, A., 1, 7, 81, 94, 95, 96, 169, 170
Schroeder, E., 212
Secrétan, C., 106
Sellars, R. W., 216
Semon, R., 214
Shapley, H., 77
Sheldon, W. H., 145
Simmel, G., 159, 160
Smith, A., 54
Smith, J. A., 167
Spaulding, E. G., 216
Spaventa, B., 9
Spencer, H., 10, 14, 15, 17, 24, 28, 29–37, 38–42, 44, 75
Spinoza, B., 84
Spranger, E., 157
Stirling, J. H., 15, 126
Stirner, M., *see* Schmidt, C.
Strauss, D., 3, 4, 10
Strong, C. A., 216
Stuart, H. W., 195
Suarez, 201

Taine, H. A., 10, 45
Tarde, G., 72
Taylor, A. E., 135
Thomas Aquinas, *see* Aquinas, T.
Thomson, J. A., 80
Titchener, E. B., 83
Tracy, D. de, 9, 97, 100, 101
Trendelenburg, A., 81
Tröltsch, E., 157
Tufts, J. H., 194
Turner, W., 203
Tyndall, J., 14
Tyrrell, G., 183, 184

Urban, W. M., 208

Vacherot, E., 10
Vaihinger, H., 195
Vera, A., 9
Verworn, M., 63

Vico, G. B., 8, 161
Vogt, K., 6
Volkelt, H., 206

Wagner, R., 94, 169, 170
Walker, L. J., 203, 205
Wallace, A. R., 14, 23
Ward, J., 143
Weber, E. H., 82, 85
Weber, M., 153
Weisse, C. H., 7
Weissmann, A., 24, 37
Whewell, W., 53
Whitehead, A. N., 80, 211, 212, 219, 220
Windelband, W., 151–153
Witherspoon, J., 17
Woodbridge, F. J. E., 217
Wulf, M. de, 203
Wundt, W., 83